Dear Vaccine

Dear Vaccine

Global Voices Speak to the Pandemic

Edited by Naomi Shihab Nye,
David Hassler, and Tyler Meier

Foreword by Dr. Richard Carmona
Afterword by Ohio Governor Mike Dewine

The Kent State University Press ▣ Kent, Ohio

This publication was made possible in part
through the generous support of

Contents

Grief—That Breath Could Bring Us Death

The Clinic—*The Place We Met and Loved Each Other*

Nostalgia—*Every Day a Meditation in Remembering*

Editors' Note

The idea for the Global Vaccine Poem began on a phone call
with Arizona arts administrators in late January 2021, con-
vened by the Arizona Commission on the Arts. Acknowledg-
ing the profound challenges the pandemic presented across
all sectors of our lives, the group was working to imagine
how we could bring all of our resources—especially from
the arts and culture sector—to help meet the specter of this
particularly difficult challenge. We talked about how our
cultural civic institutions were sites of public trust—how
could we leverage this trust? We talked about the power of
the arts to make the science behind vaccine development and
vaccination outcomes more meaningful and more powerful.
We talked about how storytelling could help allay the public
health conundrum of vaccine hesitancy.

After the call, Tyler Meier, the director of the University of
Arizona Poetry Center, reached out to David Hassler, the direc-
tor of the Wick Poetry Center at Kent State University. The
Wick Poetry Center had been pioneering digital platforms and
expressive writing tools as part of their Traveling Stanzas com-
munity poetry project and interactive website. The moment
for poetry was rich. Amanda Gorman had just mesmerized the

United States with her inaugural poem for the new presidential administration, an inflection moment in a greater trend: poetry readership has been expanding in the United States, especially among younger readers from diverse backgrounds. We know the art form is simultaneously expansive and yet provides easy access for anyone to experiment with its materials of language and honesty, emotion and compression. We quickly realized that a public, participatory art project featuring poetry had a real shot at making a difference.

David reached out to celebrated poet Naomi Shihab Nye, the Poetry Foundation's Young People's Poet Laureate, and asked her about creating a model poem for the project; her enthusiasm was (and is!) infectious, and she immediately began imagining a poem on the spot and joined the project as a key collaborator. Her poem "Dear Vaccine" was the result, and it became our model for four writing prompts to invite participation in the project.

With initial financial investment from the University of Arizona and Kent State University, the Wick Poetry Center's design and development collaborators Each + Every created the project website and the project materials. In late March 2021, www.globalvaccinepoem.com went live, and we distributed cards inviting participation into the project at vaccination sites in Arizona, Ohio, and Texas.

What happened next was profound for all of us. Thousands of responses poured in not just from partner vaccination sites but from around the globe—all 50 states and more than 150 countries to date. Responses came in from grandparents and children and from people from every walk of life. In Ohio, with support from the Ohio Arts Council, our project video was featured and aired statewide at one of Governor Mike DeWine's weekly coronavirus press conferences. The "positive contagion" of the project spread by word of mouth, on social media, and with the help of many national and regional news media outlets. To date over 26,000 people have visited the website.

As you'll see in the book that follows, responses became a kind of collective picture of our experience of the pandemic and of our hopes for what might come after. The project itself became so much more than a poetry project: at times, reading the responses, it was possible to believe we'd created a virtual wishing well, or an *offrenda*—an altar where we remember what we've lost. Periodically, it felt we had a register of grievances; at other times, the responses felt like a kind of stand-in definition for what the word "hopeful" might mean. We decided to present anthology selections as closely as possible to the way they were originally submitted online to the project. Because our project website did not allow contributors to make line breaks, we encouraged them to use a slash in their text to signify a line break. We have maintained the appearance of these submissions to stay true to the urgency and intention of the authors.

If you've participated in the Global Vaccine Poem, thank you for being a part of this ever-expanding project. If you haven't, there's still time to add your voice to the eclectic and wonderful chorus at https://www.globalvaccinepoem.com/. If we've learned anything through this time, it's that we need each and every one of us.

December 2021

David Hassler
Director
Wick Poetry Center,
Kent State University

Tyler Meier
Director
University of Arizona
Poetry Center

Foreword

COVID-19
The Great Divider, Uniter and Accelerator

The work in this anthology is a much-needed literary forensic dissection of the world in disarray searching for a safe harbor. The last year and a half we have been in an undeclared war with an invisible threat that has exposed the vulnerability of our precious and ever-evolving democracy. Two and a half centuries ago, America's founding fathers envisioned a new nation without a king, governed by the people and for the people. They memorialized their thoughts on parchment circulated on horseback and announced by town criers. There was spirited, passionate debate but seemingly no purposeful misinformation or conspiracy theories to challenge the will of the people.

From 13 colonies to 50 states, in peace and frequently at war and through epidemics, pandemics, social and economic catastrophes, and—possibly our most virulent threat—the metastasizing plague of politics, we have survived. But when this first pandemic in over a century covertly challenged our divided nation at the end of 2019, we may have been at our most vulnerable time in history. As COVID-19 struck, America had been embedded in two questionable and divisive wars over two decades. We suffered a lack of timely global medical intelligence coupled with a strategic national stockpile of much-needed health-related goods that was not fully prepared to rapidly surge to the needs of the nation or the world. All of this also came at a time of a relatively new president whose disruptive words divided us and inflamed and misinformed the public. Behind it all, a nation also divided by social injustice, numerous inequities fueled by hyper-partisan malignant politics that further undermined the public confidence in its government.

We find ourselves in a perfect storm: a Darwinian moment in history where human survivability in a now divided nation is being tested by an evolving virus that seems as determined to survive as we are.

During the last 21 months, we have learned many lessons. We are grateful, but at times COVID-exhausted, depressed, and grieving for losing more than 800,000 American souls—nearly 5.4 million worldwide. There has been immeasurable mental and physical harm. We appropriately and proudly praise our frontline heroes and have developed a new understanding of "essential employees." Yes, for example, migrant workers— often immigrants—are frequently invisible in our society while harvesting our food or providing essential support services that are necessary for us to survive and thrive. COVID struck the world and brought us to our collective knees. At a time when our optimal survival depended on achieving a united front, we succumbed to partisan tribal responses fueled by elected officials whose self-serving rhetoric drove us further apart. At war against a common foe, we must always act as Americans *and* global citizens, not as partisan activists. We now long for the more predictable and uniform days of our past as we try to envision the new world order we are creating out of survival necessity. COVID may be the most potent divider, uniter, and accelerator in our global history.

COVID did unite global scientists to act selflessly to crowd-source scientific advancement of rapidly evolving medical intelligence, which accelerated understanding of this catastrophic invisible threat and the unprecedented development and production of innovative, very successful vaccines. Also, in order not to suffer economic collapse, we accelerated tele-health, telecommuting, and digital health platforms, as well as restaurant "takeout," online shopping, delivery, and remote education at all levels. Ironically, John Barry's bestselling book, *The Great Influenza: The Epic Story of the Deadliest Pandemic in History*, about the misnamed Spanish flu of 1918, is essentially the same story today. The lessons learned then were largely forgotten. Today, a century later, we were distracted and did not heed lessons of the past. History is the prologue to our future. We must memorialize and teach these experiences so as to not repeat the preventable, self-imposed errors that have negatively impacted us and the world.

This timely and seminal literary contribution will indeed serve to memorialize this painful period of our shared human history in prose and poetry that will resonate with diverse, global audiences. The battle against COVID takes place in the arm, shot by shot, but also, and perhaps even more so, in the hearts and minds of all people. While transformative, medicine alone is not enough; as this volume proves, we know the arts have a crucial role to play.

December 2021
Richard Carmona, MD, MPH, FACS
Distinguished Professor, University of Arizona
17th Surgeon General of the United States

Acknowledgments

This beautiful book and project would not exist without the support of so many! We are so grateful to the Kent State University Press for sharing our vision for this book and to the Ohio Arts Council for their generous financial support.

For early project support, we are indebted to investments from the College of Arts & Sciences at Kent State University, and the offices of the President and Provost and the College of Humanities at the University of Arizona.

Each + Every Design helped take all our wild ideas and make them presentable and user-friendly on the www. globalvaccine poem.com website and materials.

It would have been a far different project without the partnership of vaccination sites in Ohio, Arizona, and Texas, especially those on the University of Arizona and Kent State University campuses. We're enormously grateful to Chris Kopach, Marilyn Taylor, and Luis Rocha in Tucson, to Taryn Burhanna and her Kent State College of Nursing students in Kent, and to Dr. Rachel M. Pearson of San Antonio.

We are deeply grateful to our collaborator Professor Stephanie Smith at Kent State University for her generous imagination, guidance, and expertise in creating and launching this project.

Many thanks to Laura Caywood, Paola Valenzuela, Diana Delgado, Wren Awry, Gema Ornelas, Sarah Kortemeier, Leela Denver, Julie Swarstad Johnson, and Sarah Gzemski, collectively the staff at the University of Arizona Poetry Center, and to Dr. Jessica Jewell, Charles Malone, and Györgyi Mihályi at the Wick Poetry Center at Kent State University. An especially huge thanks to Györgyi Mihályi for essential logistical and administrative support to help this book come to life.

To everyone who submitted poems for the project, endless gratitude. Your experiences and generosity are the essential substance of this book.

Lastly, forever and always—thanks to our families for their enduring patience and love.

Introduction

A four-year-old boy is building a little house with colorful magnetic blocks in the windowsill. "Look at my house, it won't have any windows or doors. So COVID can't get in."

We drive past playgrounds roped off with yellow police tape. He stares longingly through the backseat window. "Ah, I miss when I was three and we could go there to play."

Buses rumble past our house all day. His favorite pastime was riding public buses. Gone. He sees drivers through the big front windows wearing masks now, and the buses look nearly empty. He says, "They must be lonely."

No wonder my husband, mom (age 93), and I felt elation driving toward a San Antonio allergy clinic to be vaccinated against COVID-19 in late January 2021. We felt like singing! An old Girl Scout camp song popped out of my mouth. Mom joined in with soprano harmony.

We wanted to embrace the elegantly tattooed Santos, dressed all in black, who stuck the needles into our grateful arms. We welcomed Moderna as a guardian angel. In the 15-minute waiting period afterward (no one present had a reaction), I stared at people carefully spaced around us. Above their masks, in their eyes, everyone looked weary. Two ladies mumbled together. They were wearing brand-new matching polka-dotted blouses for this big day. We spoke out from under our masks to one another. "Finally! Things will be better now! Less anxiety!"

Ha!

*

Shortly after receiving our own vaccinations, David Hassler, the director of the Wick Poetry Center at Kent State University, phoned me about a collaborative public poetry initiative with Tyler Meier, the director of the University of Arizona Poetry Center, which we instantly started calling "Dear Vaccine." I wrote the first stanza of the "model poem" David requested while still on the phone with him. The whole poem was turned in the next day.

We've always believed poetry is for everybody. It's our most intimate, immediate genre of expression, often experimental, often gorgeously strange, inviting lines and thoughts and descriptions that may feel personal and specific when we write them, but might, if we're lucky, turn out to have wider resonance for other people. Poetry is honest. It gives us a place to connect bits and pieces of experience. It's an open door. Sometimes we see what we were thinking much more clearly after writing the poem.

Who wouldn't want to celebrate in language this collective moment of renewed civic possibility and shared hopes following a horrible year skewed with illness, death, cancellations, economic hardships, fears and phobias, isolations, bereavements? People would have so much to say.

And indeed they have.

Dear Vaccine is a compendium of love letters to our lives. Responses from every state and so many countries started ticking in as soon as the site went up. I'd click into our website late at night to read the news I needed most—how other humans were feeling.

Deepest gratitude to everyone in the research laboratories who worked to make vaccines possible so quickly and to the troops of workers who distributed the vaccines far and wide. Nothing has been easy. Gratitude to all the healthcare workers who risked their own lives, and deepest sorrow for those who lost them. We've each been shaken by these seasons of living through a difficult pandemic, but who could have guessed we'd start to emerge into the light again with such a fractured medley of attitudes surrounding us? We've been startled by word of countless conspiracy theories abounding. Someone in my own family announced that 35,000 people had died on the spot after receiving a vaccine—a strange secret that seems to have been shared only with him. Kids in Singapore asked me through Zoom why anyone in our country would object to wearing a mask. They said, "Doesn't the governor of Texas care about his people?" Realizing I know absolutely nothing about the "governor" or similar ruler of Singapore, I told them this was a worry I surely shared.

Thank you, contributors to *Dear Vaccine*, for sharing your thoughts with us all.

When I learn, at the end of August 2021, that 93% of the students, staff, and faculty at my alma mater, Trinity University in San Antonio, are vaccinated, I think, "Sure they are. They're smart. They've always been smart." The professor friend who tells me this news says they're hoping to catch up with the other 7% very shortly.

Naomi Shihab Nye
Young People's Poet Laureate, Poetry Foundation

Dear Vaccine

Save us, dear vaccine.
Take us seriously.
We had plans.
We were going places.
Children in kindergarten.
So many voices, in chorus.
Give us our world again!
Tiny gleaming vials,
enter our cities and towns
shining your light.
Restore us to each other. ·

We liked our lives.
Maybe we didn't thank them enough.
Being able to cross streets
with people we didn't know,
pressing elevator buttons,
smiling at strangers,
standing in line to pay.
We liked standing in line
more than we pretended.

It's a quick prick in the arm.
You'll barely notice it.
It's the gas in the car,
getting us going again.
It's the turn in the road.
Face-to-face conversation
someday soon?

It's the hug. Forever,
it's the hug!

Vaccine, please make the air clean!
We went to yoga classes,
deep collective breathing,
in small rooms in cities
where we didn't even
live! How brave we were.
Vaccine, please.
Restore our lives.
Believe they were beautiful.

Naomi Shihab Nye

Lessons

What We Learned
While Alone

Oh, Covid-19, how considerate of you to cover the world, allow Planet Earth to heal. Oh, lethal bat-birthed bane, imprison us at home, until greenhouse gas emissions go the way of the dodo. You show us, oh powerful pathogen, how to drop pollution levels with ease of coconuts from palms. Oh, queen of contagion, choke poachers' breath, keep coal in their fracked holes, shutter factories and slaughterhouses. I bow to your potent power, wear facemasks to lessen your infection and gloves to keep at bay your bacillus. You, a mighty microbe of mass murder, and yet, oh, social spreader of sickness, you mend our planet. We are mere mortals waiting for your pox to pass. Oh, toxic troubadour, who has escorted dolphins to Venice's canals, coaxed wildlife to venture out, siphoned chemicals from the seas, before we destroy you, I beseech you: make us mind the earth.

Joan Beth Gerstein
Oceanside, California

From *A 21st Century Plague: Poetry from the Pandemic*, edited by Elayne Clift, University Professors Press.

We liked being able to
/ sip our coffees in the
store / while we lingered
and browsed. / Now my
mother and I chug lattes /
in the car before entering
through doors, / vanilla
and soy breaths / coating
the inside of KN95s.

Nina Palattella
Erie, Pennsylvania

Dear vaccine, we carried ourselves like precious fragile cargo: / Don't touch, don't come close. / We had to erect barriers, become invisible, / mask our faces, lose our smiles. / Won't you save us, let us bask in each other's warmth again, / cross the 6-foot distance? / Give us the hugs we missed, / the air we never thought of doubting. / Let us remember the touch of worriless hands. / Give us back the life we never knew we loved, / the mindless walking among crowds, / the shoulder-to-shoulder sitting. / Dear vaccine, we've learned our lesson. / Your absence was our punishment. / But now it's time for redemption. / It's time to live again . . . anew. / To love again . . . more deeply. / To care again . . . more sincerely.

Nisreen Yamany
Makkah, Saudi Arabia

I feel you working in my
body / and want to work
with you / to be free of
worry and stronger for
others / Dear Vaccine, teach
us what to do next / so that
we might move on / to the
next level and be immune
to thoughtlessness ⚕✦

Yahia Lababidi
Egypt and USA

Dear vaccine, you're great, and all, but / will you also cure us / of our debilitating ability / to fracture "all" / into "people like us"?

Denise Alden
Twin Cities, Minnesota

Vaccine, it's the strangers
/ I miss. The hope / I
once felt: communion, /
holy reciprocity, what /
faces can say without / a
word spoken.

Tracy Rice Weber
Hampton, Virginia

We liked being able to sing
/ In school auditoriums
and churches, / The notes
hovering harmlessly / In the
clean air, / Threads of joy
connecting us to each other.

Liz Gray
Newton, Massachusetts

Dear vaccine, I write as if you
are my friend, as if I know you,
as if we are catching up on
the past, as if we are making
plans, as if I made a purchase
and I need to exchange it, as
if all was bad before you came
on the scene. Dear vaccine,
without you, I talked to my
son every week, I met a new
group of people online. Dear
vaccine, don't take these new
connections away, don't let us
forget the preciousness of time.

Catherine Elizabeth Gamblin
Otis, Oregon

Dear vaccine, / do you see us? / We know we are insignificant / in this universe / but we want to walk on the streets / unafraid to show our smiles to others passing by. / We promise we will be kind / to nature, to our fellow trees and seas, / to the sand and rocks, / to the ants sleeping near our books. / Do you not wish to watch us sing to our kids on swings? / Do you not know how much the parks miss / the dogs as they run after a ball? / How much fun they would have jumping in a mall? / Dear vaccine, when you enter our bodies, / you will enjoy our lives / because we will be better humans.

Mosab Abu Toha
Gaza, Palestine

Don't lure us back / to the
old normal / pretending
to know / failing to bear
witness / when this life calls
for compassionate action

David J. Bodney
Tucson, Arizona

We are blooms gone dormant. /

Find the vein of blue / the center's

shy purple / in the syringe-

sharp petals of the bright, orange

Bird of Paradise / so that we

can open anew / to the sun and

to our own dazzling / and find

ourselves nectar-rich, / recipients

of beneficent visitations— / such

purposeful and beautiful bounty.

Elizabyth A. Hiscox
Fort Collins, Colorado

It's a threshold / so we
hesitate, as we so often do /
it's like no other threshold
we've ever encountered /
one we can only cross once
we have imagined something
new / from what we've
learned from loss.

Lynda Allen
Fredericksburg, Virginia

We liked going to bed / thinking of waking to the simple / pleasure of *good morning*. We liked / not being roused by the news / another of our friends / is dead. How quietly beautiful / is the ordinary sound of things / breathing: when a child falls asleep / with her head close to your ear, / when the grandfather snores in his favorite armchair. / When at last you can open the door to nothing / more urgent than the sound of wind moving / like a blessing over the cities and fields.

Luisa A. Igloria
Norfolk, Virginia

dear vaccine / don't make us
immune / to all the ways / our
world was already / virus, a doom
/ though some of us / could not
see. / when it's time to lift / our
masks, may we / each be seen / and
breathe / each other's breath / as if
it were oxygen / dear vax

Philip Metres
University Heights, Ohio

Vaccine, please find your

way up and through

every tributary of blood

and lymph, igniting our

beautiful immunity. May

the rivers that are us restore

all watersheds—both inner

and outer—so that the

earth can continue.

Alvena Gael Kirkpatrick
Ojai, California

I finally understand the meaning
of a true patriot. I look out for my
neighbors, family, and friends by
getting the shot. But care does not
stop there. Our relationship does not
define your worth. I get the shot for
every human being because we all
need to be protected and cared for.
That is how we create a healthy world
worth saving. By caring for each other.

Rivka Joseph
Cleveland, Ohio

Vaccine, please guide
us back to a life of
connection. Teach us to
hug, to grasp, to listen
closely as we watch our
friends' lips tell stories,
knowing the puffs of warm
air that seep through each
phrase and laugh are SAFE.

Suzanne Ohlmann
Seward, Nebraska

Dear vaccine / We liked kissing, I did / skin

to skin heart-soul to / finger-tip call it pulse, /

call it touch call it love in / daylight and dark—

it's / the window-shade of singleness, / lift it,

curtain, draw it, dear / vaccine—take the first

bow so / we might take a second and a next, / a

kiss, a together-ride, a touch— / we're waiting

for your shine inside / our bodies, now, / kick

our hearts high, to kiss / again when you have

danced inside / us—we liked kissing, I did—

/ make us well for one another, / vaccine, no

more terrible / shadows, no more terrible /

landings, vaccine, believe / in our lives, kiss us,

please! / xxx, mb. /

Margo Berdeshevsky
Paris, France

Dear vaccine, please accept our
thanks in advance for lessons
we did not know we needed to
remember: touching a hand, seeing
a beloved face, giving and receiving
a true embrace. Heartbeat to
heartbeat.

Sean Dennison
Medford, Oregon

We liked being able to hold

hands and offer prayer

across the dining table with

strangers / fall asleep on a

fellow passenger's shoulder,

unintentionally / fear less for

the pieces of our heart yet

unborn / do more with our

ordinary lives / pray at our

temples with a crescendo of

chants / listen to the sounds of

silence inside museums / sleep

on unknown beds and inhale

unknown scents with abandon

Kashiana Singh
Chicago, Illinois

As we enter our new lives
/ will we remember / the
faster we moved / the sicker
we got? / Will we remember
/ not wearing our true faces?

Michael Simms
Pittsburgh, Pennsylvania

With a flip of that well-thumbed calendar / hanging on your fading walls / you realize / that it has been a year / since your weekend retreat turned refuge. / That four seasons have swept the world / beyond the square that's framed by your window / that the tentative pause / marked by your expectant semicolon / has curled itself into a period. / (A period to start your sentence.) / The slow glide of a bead of sweat / tracing your brows and mapping your face / makes you want for a human touch / but it stops at your cheeks. Soaks. / And you realize / that it has been a year / since you veiled your smile / and muffled your laugh. / You have lived a year out of history's most dreaded pages, / but now you can nudge the clock again. / A year's worth of effort and prayer is here / bottled in vials / like the elixirs of yore. / Could its mild sting set time straight again? / You choose to believe it would. / You know / it's the brush of fingers before you hold hands / it's the gentle caress before you cling to a hug / it's the soft sigh before a tender kiss / it's your year of pain, tears and bottled hope. / You savor the respite / and you know / (that the period was not to end your sentence / it was a pause before the ellipses) / it's the last stop before you come home.

TC Nivedita
Kerala, India

I've learned how much I love to be alone, / how much I've loved being alone together. / Still, it will be good to be back in the world / when we're ready, when it's safe, secure / in knowing that, even untethered, the space / between us was always its own kind of love.

Paula J. Lambert
Columbus, Ohio

Dear vaccine, there has been so much sadness, so much loneliness . . . so much death over the past year. Thanks to you and the people who created you, we see a light . . . an opportunity for us to get back to what we once were. But more than just getting back to normal, I hope your chemistry allows each and every one of us to reflect and really think about how small we are in the grand scheme of things. That we truly are all one people who need each other to survive . . . to flourish . . . together. And, that this one people mentality can help us eradicate such hate in our world and all of those things that divide us. So while I am grateful for what you have been designed to do, I am hopeful that your chemistry brings us a little bit more . . . more love, more hugs and the ability for us to listen and respect one another so we all can be a little bit more for each other.

Todd Snider
Munroe Falls, Ohio

I never thought I'd miss /
my nemesis: airport security.
The line snaking around
/ stretched end to end / it
would be miles / miles of
cranky kids, tired travelers,
dropped sippy cups, mouse
ears, and "Where'd you put
the passports??" / but I'm
ready now / ready to board
the plane to Anywhere.

Kari Wimbish
Charlotte, North Carolina

Dear vaccine, how I have missed hugging people. (To be honest, I have - against protocols - hugged my elderly parents a couple of times over the past year. It was important to have some touch. I have otherwise been very safe about masking, handwashing, physical distancing, etc.) / Dear vaccine, how I have missed singing with other people: Christmas carols, belting out weird Warren Zevon lyrics, pulling down harmonies from the ether. / Dear vaccine, this may be spoken like the Unitarian I am, but please help us all to remember that we are interconnected and mutually dependent, and may remembering that help us to be kinder to and more patient with each other, and more mindful of this fragile planet we share.

Kelley Alison Smith
Rhode Island

It's the times we spent together, the times we hugged each other, the times we could breathe freely, the times we could stand closely. Those were what we took for granted, now those were the things we wanted. This is a reminder for everyone, let your happiness yet, come.

Tan Zi Ning
Singapore

Vaccine please, help us to
learn to have compassion
for each other, to have a new
awareness of the needs of
others, to take care of each
other and this beautiful
living earth with new vision
and renewed dedication . . .
knowing you have opened the
door to another chance to get
this being human thing right
. . . or at least better.

Melissa Standish
Houston, Texas

It's the changing of the
seasons / and those everyday
moments of simple beauty
/ the gentle spring shower
of serviceberry petals / the
majesty of a hobblebush thicket
/ the promise of a kiss / In
these moments, contemplating
beauty / it is easy to forget that
the world has moved on / One
day, perhaps sometime soon /
we will have the opportunity to
see the world move on yet again
/ I will keep my heart open /
and remember this season

Eleni Hines
Black River, New Brunswick

but remind us, vaccine, of
what we learned while alone,
while behind masks and glass
doors, longing for all that was.
Remind us of the ways we leaned
toward one another, how we
found ways to help, to send love
across distance, welcome the
newly born, shout out to the
lonely, heal our emptiness. Dear
vaccine, help us remember even
in your new and welcome safety

Ann N. Vermel
Fort Collins, Colorado

Dear vaccine, you come / in your fancy names: Pfizer, / Moderna, AstraZeneca, / Johnson & Johnson (some- / times the names are not / so fancy). Somewhere / as you read this, a man / or woman is dreaming / in their dream laboratory / of saving the world / from ourselves, and our / brilliant and complicated / ways. It's an experiment, / the simple task of going / about our days, practicing / gratitude. Praise the science / and joy in becoming / what we were: something / old, familiar, and new.

Ken Waldman
Anchorage, Alaska

Oh, I never thought, dear vaccine, / I would ever need ya / so sure was I / of playing the percentages / roaming unmasked / arrogant and cocky. / It was my daughter, / dear vaccine, / who said, "Pop, you're 71 / you could die. / I can't lose you." / You're right, dear Daughter / as you have always been. / Two shots later / and she is relieved / as I've never seen her. / Dear vaccine, my daughter / is awesome.

Marc A. Crowley
Cochise County, Arizona

Gratitude

Only as Lovely as You Are Shared

Dear vaccine, I waited for
your touch, a lover's touch
/ tender, gentle, freeing me
from bondage / freeing me to
embrace, to gather, to hold
hands / your touch removed my
fear / opened my heart / opened
my doors / opened my life to
the world / this fragile world
forever changed / perhaps wiser
and perhaps kinder

Dorothy Beavington
Surrey, British Columbia, Canada

Dear vaccine / Kulañ, ṣa: ʼap aʼi masma: We
meet you and shake your hand in greeting. / It
has been some time since we shook anyone's
hand. / S-ap ʼac t-taːtc ia m-ñei. / We are happy
to see you. / Hekihu amjeḍ ʼac ʼia m-ñenḍa. /
We have been waiting for your arrival for some
time. / Your journey is done you will now rest
in our bodies. / Like other healers before you /
you will be there when we need you. / The tale
of your journey will be held in our collective
stories. / We will retell it next year when we
acknowledge the death anniversaries / of our
relatives and friends and all those who tried
to fight the enemy alone. / We will tell of the
battles you fought on your journey / the battles
against non-believers and conspiracy theorists.
/ You will be known as a hero, a slayer of
enemies. / And like so many others before you /
you will be known by many names.

Ofelia Zepeda
Tucson, Arizona

Today my torch cactus burst
into flower, seven yellow
trumpets, a forte of sweet
music, telling the bees to
come on over and taste the
nectar. That's just how it
feels to get a shot of good
medicine in the arm and
meet your beloveds for a
drink and toast, the life we
love so much we sing now of
mRNA and science, feeling
our bodies become tuned
once again to each other.

Alison Hawthorne Deming
Tucson, Arizona

Dear vaccine, / we praise the scientists / who worked overtime / to bring you into being / to give us a chance / at more life / more hugs / more singing / more hands in delicious dirt / transplanting lettuces. // While we were sheltered in place, / scientists sheltered in labs / focused on their intricate / saving work to bring you to us. / Vaccine, I give you my arm. / And through their faithfulness / you give me back my life.

George Ella Lyon
Lexington, Kentucky

Oh, the ache in the arm / is love / the woozy day after / is love / the immunity / is love. Oh my darling / oh my darling / oh my darling vaccine.

Carl Little
Somesville, Maine

Let us gather

upcloseandpersonal

where miracles happen

Candace Frede
New York, New York

Dear vaccine, look
at the fresh snow
purifying the air
of the city, a late
snow covering
spring flowers, yet
letting us breathe,
a welcome pause,
just like the one
you shall bring,
as I hope, for the
new spring to
bloom it this city
on Earth.

Anna Mari Räsänen
Helsinki, Finland

Dear vaccine, on behalf of old
vaccinated people everywhere
. . . last night . . . I dropped a line
to Death, . . . that arbiter of time,
. . . that preachy and insatiable
realist, . . . and said, . . . Step back,
recalculate, . . . O taskmaster of the
soul. . . . Not so fast, not so fast.

Mary Zettelman Greer
Shalersville, Ohio

It's a bird song in the morning after a night of storms. / It's a new bud on the basswood tree after winter's hibernation. / It's a fragile shoot that promises the flowers of spring.

Suzanne Kilkus
Madison, Wisconsin

It's the spring in my tired step; / the smile behind my mask; / the hope in each exhalation; / it's the wondrous world of loud laughter between my parents in Germany and me in America after our dark, cold, long winter. / Let the rebuilding begin.

Silke Feltz
Norman, Oklahoma

47

Vaccine, please
bring back our
dancing shoes,
and we will
sing our song of
freedom. We will
hold hands and
do a jig across
the land in our
extravagant
gratitude and
bless your pointy
head.

Fran Hillyer
Glorieta, New Mexico

Dear vaccine, keep showing us
your brightest side, be gentle, be
generous and don't be like us.
You bring hope to a tired flock
that lost way too much over the
last year. And as I say 'grazie' and
caress my left arm I think of the
still too many that cannot afford
your touch. Come in thousands,
in millions, in billions: overcome
borders and barriers, and meet all
of those who need you more.

Fabio Corsini
Rome, Italy

Dear vaccine, / We have been waiting
for you / Ready to roll up our sleeves to
receive you / Smiling behind our masks
in anticipation / Of your gentle piercing
// And although some people are afraid
of you / Cannot bring themselves to trust
you / As if the virus is their friend! / As if
this pandemic that has killed millions /
Is less of a threat? / Just a hoax invented
by some fool! / Please ignore them / They
will eventually come around / Or perhaps
they are hoping to survive long enough /
For the rest of us to save them // Yes, dear
vaccine / You are the savior / Come sing
us / Your molecular song / Of freedom.

Lahab Assef Al-Jundi
San Antonio, Texas

It's the thing to do. Be a good citizen, it's the neighborly thing to do. It's the right thing to do. It's the thing to do to be with my friends, family and fellow citizens. It's the right thing to do, so just go do the vaccination tango! Let's dance.

Dean R. Kahler
Canton, Ohio

Dear vaccine, each
sacrifice, large or small,
each loss, large or small,
was on the road to you,
guided by people who
believed in the value of
human life

Konrad Ng
Honolulu, Hawaii

Dear vaccine, You can't save us from the losses we have already endured. You can't save us from the war against black bodies. You can't end racism, ethnocentrism, xenophobia, white supremacy, greed, and violence. BUT . . . you, vaccine, can allow us to safely gather again, to mourn and grieve together. To create and innovate as a community. To uplift and empower with proximity and embrace. You can restore the closeness that our humanity longs for.

Samantha Antoine
Ann Arbor, Michigan

Dear vaccine, Thank you! / Thank you in advance for providing hope and possibilities / Thank you for pushing back against death, mourning and despair / Thank you for healing / Thank you for saving / Thank you for life / Dear vaccine, Thank you! / Thank you for listening to the struggle of the people / Thank you for hearing the voice of humanity / Thank you for giving me time . . . / . . . time to love, / . . . time to hold, / . . . time to hug / Dear vaccine, Thank you! / Thank you for allowing me to re-enter the world / Not as I was before / But . . . with much resolve, / with more faith, / with more fight, / with more hope / Dear vaccine, Thank you / Thank you for traveling the earth / Thank you for opening up the future to / . . . to the children of the world / . . . to my children / — to us all.

Amoaba Gooden
Kent, Ohio

Dear vaccine, we
marvel at whatever
/ is happening deep
inside / our cells
being schooled / by a
few drops of miracle /

Kate McCarroll Moore
Danville, California

It's the song of tomorrow /
our voices inhale to sing / the
only sustenance for the fear /
which has usurped hope / from
humanity. / It's the reason to live
again / if we're questioning why /
as a herd locks fingertips. / It's the
way we'll resuscitate / our hearts.
They need a vaccine, / too, but,
you, our friend start our journey.

Susan M. Tyrrell
Lawton, Oklahoma

Dear vaccine, I am so grateful for you. Thank you for the relief you have brought to me and to those I love. My heart wants to hug you and sing you a love song!

Tish Hinojosa
Austin, Texas

Dear vaccine,
you are only as lovely
as you are shared
with all the people of
the world

Sue Soal
Cape Town, South Africa

On earth, as it is in the
bloodstream / give us motion
and color, give us waves / of
light and we promise to take
even / the smallest things
seriously. Oh vaccine, / with
your mysterious spelling, we
/ thank you down to the last
double C / of us.

Brendan Constantine
Los Angeles, California

It's the invisible cloak we can wear for protection / Its power lies in the tightness of the weave / Every stitch carries a name

Emily-Sue Sloane
Huntington Station, New York

Dear vaccine,
you slip in like / a
double agent / tiny /
invisible / the body
can go / back to
routine / while you
keep watch / around
the perimeter

Susan Scheid
Washington, DC

Dear vaccine, / you are a pointy oxymoron: / you break the skin to heal the body, / kill an illness to save the world, / you are the contradiction and the solution.

Muna Agwa
Cleveland, Ohio

Dear vaccine: I love everything about

you. Every. last. thing. Your scientists and

researchers with their decades of study of other

deadly diseases. Your novel structure. Your

volunteers helping administer you to me. Your

mass vaccination sites that sprang up overnight

in my city. Your speedy invention. Your

startling efficacy. Your friendly nurse handling

your vial at the window of my car. Your sharp

poke. Your little card that says: I've got you.

The sore arm waking me in the night, a kid on

Christmas morning, reminding me of all the

hugs I'm almost ready to give.

Kate Sommers-Dawes
San Francisco, California

Dear COVID-19, each of us will not forget how **we felt before** you arrived. Our memory is stronger than your destruction. And that is a blessing.

Bill Bradley
New York City, New York

Throw open the wind- / ows
- I'm learning to love all / of
my enemies –

TC Tolbert
Tucson, Arizona

Vaccine, please be

/ kind to Black and

Brown bodies / who

have already endured

/ so much

Kami Bates
Tucson, Arizona

Dear vaccine,

please don't be shy. I am / or

dare I say we are / so very,

very eager to get to know

you. / To welcome you / first

into our temple-selves /

then into our lives entire.

Emily Gammons
Columbus, Ohio

Dear vaccine,
I meant to write sooner,
vaccine to introduce
you to my blood, to my
fears I mean to touch to
breath easier, you have
come just in time for
time has come

Jenny Browne
San Antonio, Texas

This at-risk nurse's head and heart reaches out to touch your body and soul, oh human being, COVID or not!

Susan Markovich
Waterloo, Iowa, and Tucson, Arizona

dear vaccine,

you were a missing

spark / my body

welcomed with

shivers / then relief

/ I wish I could be

a shield, too / or an

ember / instead of

something so fragile

Sarah Gzemski
Tucson, Arizona

Vaccine, please allow
me to walk amongst
strangers, to no longer
dodge those who I come
across. It's those little
unexpected interactions
with others that help to
make us whole.

Lindsay Mann
Ann Arbor, Michigan

Grief

That Breath Could
Bring Us Death

As I roll up my
sleeve for you,
dear vaccine,
I pray. Please,
save us from
ourselves.

Melanie Miller
Columbus, Ohio

None of us
imagined that
breath / could
bring us death
/ as we sat, rapt,
in a darkened /
theater watching
shadows on the
screen.

Robbi Nester
Lake Forest, California

Dear vaccine, please help us fools

/ in sweatpants stop / avoiding eye

contact / and going mute behind

/ our masks. Please comfort / the

quarantined old / woman who keeps

/ asking, "What did I / do wrong?"

Please cure / Walmart panic. We are

/ writing our pandemic / stories in

third person / and blessing curbside

/ library. Can you help us / be like

the taiko drummer / who everyday

climbs / the peak and summons /

the dawn? Can you please?

Meg Files
Tucson, Arizona

O dear vaccine: The cooks are sent home,
our maid's in-laws are too ill—are taken
to hospital; now, at the Towers, they
drop our meals behind the door. O dear
vaccine, I return to the stationary bike;
sick of the cable news, leftover food.
Texting, taking a selfie, banging my head
against the wall. O dear vaccine, I am a
sweaty prisoner in a hole, I swallow a
sleeping pill every night. Come, enter my
warm arm. Visit me again in a month,
help me to travel & visit my grandchild.

Mo H. Saidi
San Antonio, Texas

Yellow Peril is on the rise. Fear of it never dies. / With our slanted eyes, yellow skin, we never did fit in. / Speaking tones discordant to their ears, fear of us never disappears. / They coveted the things we made—paper, gun powder, tea, carved jade—raced to open our shores to trade. / They sweetened the deal with the flower of addiction. / They hastened the fall of the Middle Kingdom— bloated, teetering and decadent— grabbed what they could with contempt. / We watched the exodus of our neighbors, the migration of cheap labor. / Segregated in shacks along railroad tracks, deprived of wives and confined to women's work, / our men were shunned as feminine. Sipping opium draughts in dream-smoke dens, / a cure for homesickness, / our habits were deemed degenerate, unseen the loneliness. / They tried to keep us out. / They harassed, passed laws, burned down our tenements. / Amid fears that the mongrel hordes would taint the national skin, we slipped in, / became model citizens, swore allegiance, spoke when spoken to our best English. / Corralled behind barbed wire after confiscating our property, our sons enlisted to prove to one country our loyalty. / The fumbled war exploded nightly on the news, crimes my family knew / would be forgiven. To them we were just gooks. We all looked alike. Torching villages, they went berserk, / stringing into necklaces ears and fingers of the enemy. / The invasion brought jobs, neon-bar girls in red-light districts, a nascent sex industry. / We watched Saigon fall, the evacuation of the embassy, transport planes lifting the last cargo of refugees. / So many dust children were left behind, fatherless. / A living buddha's act of self-immolation, a terrible kindness. / Like the virus circulating in caves, Yellow Peril remained contained until a cough, a sneeze bloomed fear into blame. / Suspect now are the things we eat, / our predilection for the wildest meat, where the boundary between beast / and man—our common human appetite— collides on the fatal butcher's block. / The virus jumped from bat to civet cat, perhaps / even the endangered pangolin. Never mind reason or origin—a bone for broth or an exotic delicacy— what hasn't been done, stolen or given, throughout our entangled history?

Cathy Song
Volcano, Hawaii

Dear vaccine,

you save us as much

as you scare us / We

need you as much as

we fear you / We loved

you as much as we love

our freedom / And

now we suspect you as

much as we suspect our

governments . . . / That is

the ambivalence we feel

in times of COVID-19

Jade Busca
Marseille, France

Dear vaccine, you
shot into my arm
on the mouth of
my angel tattoo.
Right on the
kisser, vaccine.
The angel's
message is always
fear not. Now, dear
vaccine, I can
heed her good
tidings.

Katherine Willis Pershey
Western Springs, Illinois

It's the short, sharp pain—
a welcomed feeling after a
year of dull ache. Memories
of a sugar cube soaked with
medicine.

Todd Diacon
Kent, Ohio

Now for over a whole long year / We lived

like prisoners, in a lot of fear / Not kissing

or hugging our kin and friends / Distancing,

wearing masks, washing hands, the trends /

Have we ever appreciated enough the bliss /

Of a gentle touch, of a hug or a kiss? / COVID!

True you cleaned the skies / But took away

so many dear lives / We are so grateful to the

Front Liners' will / Who sacrificed their lives to

save the ill / And now you have come our dear

vaccine / Hopefully to rebuild the shattered

scene / We welcome your tiny pricks to save /

And pray to our Maker to remove the wave.

Shihab M. A. Ghanem
Dubai, United Arab Emirates

Dear vaccine, make school a safe place again. / We knew that, for some, school was / a haven, a home, a hope. / We know that now, for all, school is / a vulnerability, a venture, a variant. / Dear vaccine . . . please make school safe again.

Ellyse Theede
Saskatoon, Saskatchewan, Canada

it's the only choice

for most, but not so

for those who mean

most to me // they toe

the line and i hold my

breath, hoping that

they hold on to theirs

Aleksandra Golos
Philadelphia, Pennsylvania

I wonder why my thrift store top has a fake zipper for a pocket decoration. The pocket is sewed shut. I wonder why my friend of thirty years won't get vaccinated. I can return the top but what do I do with my friend?

Joanne Feenstra
Slocan, British Columbia, Canada

I feared for myself /

I feared for the most

vulnerable / now that

they are reaching safety

/ I fear for the ones that

do not want it

Hannah Potter
Pasadena, Maryland

Dear vaccine, restore us to each other. / Rescue us from this sea in which we are drowning, / drowning in loss of loved ones, relationships, and hope. / Bring my head out from under the water, / let us breathe again, / as you let us gasp for air and catch our breath. / Guide us to land, dear vaccine.

Vivian Blatnik
Kent, Ohio

It's the waiting for months—while others get it—until my turn and then yours. Then it's the waiting for the second one. And the hope, waiting and hope. It's all of us in this together. It's the fear then the waiting then the hope.

Terri Pilarski
Dearborn, Michigan

It's the kiss that
wakes us from our
year's long sleep /
the fairy godmother
sending us back to
the ball

Gail Rinderknecht
Shaker Heights, Ohio

Dear vaccine,
you gave me my first
peace / in a year. With
one shot, I / walked
away feeling like the
world might / spin
aright on its axis once
more. / It had stopped,
you know: / Dad, Jim,
Dick, Stephan, Peggy,
Phil, Connie, Kim . . .
all gone. / You arrived
in time for me, but too
late for them.

Bonnie James Shaker
Burton, Ohio

Dear vaccine,

you came too late for my

grandmother / but just in

time for my nephew / thank

you for letting me finally

hold him / and I can feel her

life anew

Erin Kearney
Kitchener, Ontario, Canada

We liked spontaneous road trips without risk assessment and strategic planning—how long can I go without a bathroom break, how much of this coffee can I drink? We liked the thought of sewing and baking with our mom, even if we didn't visit as often as we should, and now we worry that we missed our opportunity. Lots of things stood still for the pandemic, but Parkinson's wasn't one of them.

Sandra Villeneuve
Ottawa, Canada

Dear vaccine,
if my mother were alive
/ she'd be pushing her
walker through the line
up / for a taste of you /
if my sister were alive
/ she'd be saying don't
hesitate / go, drink of
this cup / if my father,
who survived the war,
were alive he'd be
standing in line on his
tired legs / grateful and
weeping.

Genevieve Lehr
Halifax, Nova Scotia, Canada

Bless you for coming to us. You are our most important guest. Stay with us. Tell us stories of the lives you have saved, where you have been and where you are going. You bring us freedom and confidence to go forward. Weep with us for those for whom you were too late. But in their names, we take you in and honor you and each other.

Julie Heifetz
Rockville, Maryland

It's the so-called first world

that will be saved / here in

other nations we wait in line

/ we yearn to be seen

Tanya Huntington
Mexico City, Mexico

Dear vaccine, / It's too late for Vahab / But you can save his wife and daughter. / They still water his roses / And feed his canaries / But cannot watch his last video again / When he tried to teach his class on Zoom / And his coughs were more than his words.

Majid Naficy
Los Angeles, California

Dear vaccine,

you were too late for
Uncle Al / but please
spread your safety faster
/ than the variants'
gurgling appetite / Please
convince the naysayers to
expose their shoulders /
before they expose their
families. / Godspeed.

Peter Kahn
Chicago, Illinois

Dear vaccine, / Please save someone else's grandma since you were too late to save mine / A day after her funeral you were in the local news / My mother crumpled on the couch, holding the paper to her chest / You finally made it to grandma's nursing home / Please save the rest of them

Sadie Schlegel
Holmesville, Ohio

My dear vaccine, thank you.
/ In five weeks I will be able
to hug my 91 year old father. /
In five weeks I will be able to
kiss his scruffy cheek. / In five
weeks I will be able to see him
for the first time / in over a
year, see him for the first time
/ since his wife of sixty-seven
years died. / My mother, my
hub. And we will laugh and cry
/ as we pore over photographs,
as we / tell stories and
remember the time . . . / finally.

Julie Naslund
Bend, Oregon

Oh dear vaccine.
My niece / is
more afraid of
you / than of the
virus. / How can I
let her know / you
are her protector,
/ her seatbelt in
this speeding
car? / You can't
prevent a wreck,
but / if she does
crash / you're her
best hope.

Peggy Shumaker
Fairbanks, Alaska

Dear vaccine, I wish you existed one week earlier / so that you could pierce my grandma's thin skin / I hope people take you seriously / I have a life to live / the next stage of my life without her / but possible because of you

Hailey Schlegel
Holmesville, Ohio

The Clinic

The Place We Met and
Loved Each Other

At the vaccination clinic / blue stickers

mark six-foot intervals / on worn,

conference-centre carpet— / round,

like happy faces, but with feet / where

mouths should be. / The man ahead

of me wears flip-flops, / toes bare,

reddened, curling up / at the edges

when he walks, / tic toc, slip slap. / I.D.

cards—not empty bowls—outheld, /

we shuffle in snaking lines, follow / the

pointing arm of a Red Cross Knight. /

He herds us to lance-wielding nurses

/ who jab us each alone. We wait / for

immunity—for grace.

Jodi Lundgren
Victoria/Lekwungen, British Columbia, Canada

The pharmacist said
"think happy thoughts"
as the needle went
in / Dear vaccine, my
happiness will be the
deep breaths I haven't
been able to take since
December / And the
energy to be myself again
/ You are the literal shot
in the arm I need to get
my life back

Stephanie Vincent
New Castle, Pennsylvania

It's a memory we'll share in years to come, / pointing to the place we got it, left or right / arm, mostly, and the places we got it: / fairground, racetrack, old K-Mart or Sears, / school gymnasium, church parking lot, / rural grange hall, shuttered restaurant— / the places we met and loved each other.

Lynn Otto
Oregon

I trust science, and I trust you. But I'm
not sure how fully I believe in you.
I made the choice to be vaccinated,
but I felt I had no choice. How else
am I to keep myself, my family, my
students safe? So here we are, card in
hand. I stretch my arm and know it
could be worse. So much worse. Will
this cautious optimism let me see
my parents again? Will there be a day
when my children don't ask "Do we
need a mask?" They buckle up, hands
out for sanitizer / trained so well for
this circumstance they shouldn't have
to endure. Yet here we are / In a place
we were unprepared to be. Wash for 20
seconds / and wait to be free.

Teresa Anthofer
Tucson, Arizona

It's the long, long
line forming /
communion-like
outside the church
door, / parishioners
now waiting silently
while masked, / so
grateful for a needle
in the arm / rather
than the wafer on
the tongue.

Mark Scheel
Mission, Kansas

Dear Vaccine,

you brought us / from small Maine
towns / to the new arena in Bangor /
where in late winter / we once traveled
/ over frost heaved roads / to watch our
basketball teams / in the state tourney. /
Now we gather again and line up, / not
to head to the stands and cheer, / but to
have smiling (if I could see / inside their
masks) volunteers / direct us to you. To
let you / journey inside us to places too /
small for us to see / and too large for us
/ to comprehend. / Dear Vaccine, we roll
up our sleeves / or take off our shirts, /
we think of those who / are no longer
here, we think / of the places we have
come from / and our road home.

Stuart Kestenbaum
Deer Isle, Maine

We made idle chatter / "I like your tattoo" / "That's some wind out there" / "I almost said your temp was *seventy*-eight, ha!" / But when the needle went in / we went silent / with hope.

Sean Petrie
Austin, Texas

It's the lines of us in
gymnasiums / where friends
held roller skating parties
/ waiting with our sleeves
rolled / the volunteers who
smile above their masks
and tick clipboards / the
shape of the shoulders of
the gentleman in front / the
relief of his pulse slowing to
'I like to live' / Outside two
ladies stand holding hands
laughing with relief, while
the sky carries on anyway.

Hannah Jane Walker
Cambridge, United Kingdom

Some people there were that wouldn't take vaccines. At bars and restaurants we'd find them there. They were all wine and sneeze, and we for public safety. We kept the mask between us as we went. We thought the CDC messages to them would never get across, but now at spring mending-time we find them in line. We say, "The vaccinated make good neighbors."

Steven Oscherwitz
Tucson, Arizona

Second shot at the pharmacy, waiting my turn in the aisle of greeting cards—between "Get Well Soon" and "Son / Birthday / Funny"—I love the old lady bowing over her older mother crumpled into a chair. I love the frumpy codger in robe and slippers. I love the feeble couple leaning together like trees. I love the athlete dressed for running and bantering with strangers. I love "Is this the line? . . . Are you next? . . . Take my seat." And oh how I love the pharmacist, Asian-American in white coat, blue gloves, telling me his older parents are still safe, but far—as he so deftly jabs my eager arm, and I rise under florescence to thread my way through this lovely world.

Kim Stafford
Portland, Oregon

Do not hug your vaccinator
/ though the urge is strong
and true— / front line staff
aren't trained to cater /
for your excess gratitude
/ Do not promise lifelong
ardour / Don't genuflect
while in the queue / Do not
make the process harder /
Do bare your arm then say
adieu / Do not call them
Blessed Saviour / Do not
attempt to shine their
shoes / Do get a grip—and
maybe later / pen a grateful
ode or two

Jacqueline Saphra
London, United Kingdom

Smiling my thanksgiving under a
mask / The efficient receptionist
who took my form / The volunteer
who showed me where to proceed
/ Thank you to the nurse , with
her kind voice / Thank you to
the makers of alcohol swabs for
cleaning the site on my left arm. /
I am grateful for the pharmacist,
drawing up the exact dose / the
fine painless needle, where was
it made I wonder? / The brilliant
researchers in their labs day and
night developing the vaccines /
Fifteen minutes to reflect, then out
to my waiting husband and feeling
the sunlight on my shoulders. /
Next recipient in line . . .

Elizabeth Gillespie
London, Ontario, Canada

An elderly friend searched
for weeks, then found a
pharmacy with a few extra
doses in a small town that
is a three-hour drive from
his home. He drove there
immediately although he
seldom drove that far for any
reason. Later he said he felt
great during the drive, as if
he had won some great prize,
and just had to come to pick
it up in person.

Warren Woessner
Minneapolis, Minnesota

It's the hour and a half

of patient anticipation

/ My arm turned out to

be just another tricep

for stabbing / To the

blue-gloved hand / That

I wanted to shake and

shake and shake again

Bruce Gungle
Tucson, Arizona

Dear vaccine, I am watching the nurse, / lift the small vial of you, / clear as any cloudless sky. / Because we have the cow / to thank for your name, dear vaccine, / I am picturing four or five / Red Angus in a long-grassed field, / unfettered as the few good / decisions I have made. / The nurse lifts the syringe, / then dabs my arm, / dear vaccine –and there's / one cow in particular / standing by the weather-worn / post and rail fence, the kind / that lined the fields of my childhood. / And this bovine's eyes, / shine like the pond / where we'd dunk ourselves / to ease the sweltering days, / lying afterwards, side by side / on the warm granite slab. / Dear vaccine, I'm remembering / one afternoon, when Lila / nearly drowned, and Father dove in, / dove down and pulled her up, / blued but coughing / and we all cried with the kind of relief / we'd never felt before. / I watched the nurse, dear vaccine, / and thanked her, and thanked her, / and thanked her once more.

Sally Bliumis-Dunn
Armonk, New York

It's the silvery, disco-ball band aid
that the young nursing student sticks
to my upper arm that gives me hope.
/ The next steps still feel shaky with
fear. / But this token of the vaccine
(and my privilege in getting one)
has echoes of dancing feet, colorful
clothing, looser limbs, freer thoughts
and physical proximity. / I want to
celebrate. Can we celebrate yet?

Barbara Solow
Florence, Massachusetts

Dear vaccine, I had to meet you. / If not for me, for them – for my grandma, who I used to / laugh and cry with over a bowl of oatmeal, / for my little cousin always asking when / the next family get-together would be, / for my mom, afraid she might pass out in her kitchen / and awake in a hospital. // I stood in a long line with others / waiting for your pinch in my arm. / The lady ahead of me who looked like my grandma / in her purple suit and a big hat shouted, / "I'm going to church after this," / then graciously gave you her arm. // Each tiny syringe of you contains / the power to bring the world together. // We're getting closer to our Sunday gatherings / and family cookouts, / hi-fives, daps, and hugs. // With you, dear vaccine, / it grows easier by the day. / I am so glad I met you. / If not for me, for them.

Isaiah Hunt
Cleveland, Ohio

Nostalgia

Every Day a Meditation
in Remembering

Dear vaccine, I miss our kind. Remember how awkward we were? Too many people in a small café. Bumping into someone saying I'm sorry. Spilling popcorn on a stranger in the dark. We didn't know how much we needed each other. Dear vaccine, women once had names like yours: Maxine, Doreen, and Bernadine, which means "strong as a bear." I imagine you lumbering through the wilds of our cellular forests, showing the way through thickets of berries to fish-filled lakes. Oh, lead us back to the wilderness of touch, back into each other's arms. Take us to our green and possible life.

Danusha Laméris
Santa Cruz, California

We liked when breathing didn't
feel like gambling / being able to
see the small lines around your
mouth when smiling. / We liked
the world that still contained
the people we've lost / being
able sing loudly and without
reservation, unworried that the
song contained anything more
than spirit and music.

Carrie Newcomer
Bloomington, Indiana

I didn't know / how much
I loved to touch / the mail,
library books, handrails / on
the city bus. Or to sit there
/ beside a stranger, sharing /
our breath / in that moving
space. Vaccine, / restore us /
to our momentary kinship.

Julie Swarstad Johnson
Tucson, Arizona

We liked being able to high-five / or give a quick hug / to people we don't know well / in a moment of shared grace / that makes the flowers grow.

Parker J. Palmer
Madison, Wisconsin

We liked being able to breathe in our bubbe's scent, slurp her familiar spaghetti, play with the dial on her bedroom radio, hug a long time at the door.

Linda C. Belans
Durham, North Carolina

We liked carrying our groceries home by backpack after walking to and from the store most days / Being able to take advantage of sale prices and enjoy the freshest produce / Instead of weekly online orders picked by strangers and collected by car. / We liked meeting friends at a museum / Being able to whisper about colours and lines and the play of light / Instead of making the best of yet another Zoom call with freeze ups and lag. / We liked dining out once or twice a month / Being able to try new-to-us or favourite menu items while taking a break from the kitchen / Instead of planning and cooking the 442nd supper in a row. / We liked hugging family and friends who don't share our roof / Being able to squeeze tight before stepping back to grin with joy / Instead of sending v-hugs and waving awkwardly from 2 meters away.

Denise Kitagawa
Calgary, Alberta, Canada

We liked seeing faces we liked seeing
teeth. Gums full of spinach and pink
rosey cheeks. We liked seeing noses with
bats in the caves, freckles and stubble
and smooth morning shaves. All public
relations reduced to the eyes. Strangers
seem stranger beneath the disguise. Missed
shared expressions from others in line.
Attempting to stand out by way of design.
Vaccines will deliver that world of BC. Tear
off that mask, please come close, let me see.

Tina McGill
London, Ontario, Canada

Dear Vaccine / . . . Give back the wobbly table / at the front of my physical classroom, / where students and I broke bread, read / a braided essay as snow fell out our window. / . . . Let elders more time to speak in Diné, / and Mi'kmaq and Haida: voices not muted / by hospital glass but heard laughing / shoulder-to-shoulder. / . . . Grant us the perfume of a crowded opera, / the useful liberty of shared work / the sacred plume of chalk dust, saw dust, pollen, / dandelion butter on our naked noses. / . . . Allow us one more view from a 747, cheek pressed to glass to see the Rockies beneath sherbet strata of pink . . . / . . . And my second-hand quilted purse? I'd like / to carry its bright paisley back out into the world— / dive deep into its pockets for a shining dime / when a stranger can't find their own. / . . . Let us, Oh Vaccine, share / life's brief and brimming cup— / passed hand to hand / to hand. /

Jessica Jones
Ohio and Montana

Dear Vaccine, we glued our ears to the news as the body count increased on a daily basis. We became virtual prisoners in our homes and began to dread the catch phrases: 'stay at home, wash your hands, keep twenty metres apart'. We are not a city that likes being stand-offish or being socially distanced or told what to do. We are a city that greets the stranger with sayings like 'bout ye' and 'what's the craic?' Then when things were really dark, and we were facing another lockdown we heard the words 'vaccine breakthrough' and we rejoiced at words 'rollout'. We celebrated and waited like soldiers for our age group to be called up and suddenly, dear vaccine we saw light at end of the tunnel.

Brenda Liddy
Belfast, Northern Ireland

We liked watching movies in crowded theatres, even if the person behind us laughed too loudly.

Grace Nye
Melbourne, Australia

I liked being able to see
the food / stuck in between
people's teeth / I was
reassured they had at least
something to eat.

Claire Weiner
Ann Arbor, Michigan

Enough, dear vaccine, / of searching strangers' eyes / for what smiles once revealed

Sonnet Kekilia Coggins
Makawao, Hawaii

We miss surprise / conversations, without links, unscheduled, sensate. / We miss a world where anything can happen / except for what we fear the most.

Taylor Kirby
Austin, Texas

We liked sitting across from / friends in coffee shops. / We miss each other's eyes, / delighting in their sparkle. / We miss nuances of conversation, / knowing when to wait and / when to speak.

Prasanta Verma
Milwaukee, Wisconsin

Dear Vaccine, there are
so many hands to hold,
so many hugs to fill
our lonely rooms. We
remember gazing into
each other's eyes without
a screen, the sound of
children laughing, the
creak of a tree swing in the
forest, no longer forgotten,
every day a meditation in
remembering.

Marie Boucher
Monterey, California

It's the warm weight of them
in my arms / I miss most
of all / That soft skin, that
child-smell . . . Perfume
to a grandmother, / More
precious than any other.

Sophia Caparisos
Savannah, Georgia

Envisioning the Future

Believing We Belong to
the Same Beauty

Dear vaccine,

for too long I have been a goldfish circling a small bowl . . . a goose hissing at danger near my brood . . . a spider fretting, my carefully spun webs rent in this storm. At midnight, I am a mosquito playing vibrato on the e-string . . . a loon, wailing for those I cannot touch . . . a doe in strange woods, twitchy. Vaccine, please bring me back to my anthropoid self . . . a woman who wakes without dread to a day rife with possibility.

Mary Ellen Chown
Oakville, Ontario, Canada

We liked crossing invisible country borders / because we felt no borders were to pass. // Teach people trust / restore intimacy, make us robust.

Cristiana Pagliarusco
Vicenza, Italy

Vaccine, please, while you're at it, immunize us from our inclination to hurt each other by word and deed.

Dan Rosen
Kamakura, Japan

It's the vaccine needle, like a compass needle, / pointing us toward true north, / toward where we need to go. / No more losing our direction as we sit quarantined alone in silent rooms, / no more wandering aimlessly on the back roads of memories. / The future will pull us ahead to rooms bright with laughter, / to open highways that stretch their arms all the way to the gleaming horizon. / Soon our friends will lift off their masks, / and we'll recognize their faces again. / Soon we will stand in front of a mirror, / remove our own mask and say hello, again, to that person / who has been a stranger for too long--our healthy selves.

Bill Meissner
St. Cloud, Minnesota

Dear vaccine / we like to sing

and mingle / we're tiring of this

hugless life / please bring us

home / to each other's arms /

that we might warm ourselves

/ by the light of friendship's

hearth / breathing out music /

instead of heartache and death

/ and listening / to the chorus

of the world's healing / learning

again our communal lung song.

Dawn Garisch
Cape Town, South Africa

Vaccine, please, help us remember the clarity we achieved when the world was taken away from us. / Help us remember to slow down when the world speeds back up

C. Louise Kennedy
Vero Beach, Florida

Believe we deserve you / believe
our arms are ready / believe
the embraces we'll give our
grandparents / will be passed on
to their oldest friend with a sigh,
a tear / passed on to the youngest
child on the block with a chuckle,
an apple / believe all embraces will
multiply until we can hold the
moon / all of us on earth holding
moonlight all at once, / believing
we belong to the same beauty.

Barbara Ras
Denver, Colorado

Vaccine, please bring us
much light and serenity,
peaceful enlightenment
and eternity. Vaccine,
please hear my covidial
utterence. World still
waits here for me. Green
and clean my dreams still
may be. We are past and
future, but now healthy
I want to be. We are that
unwritten grammar of
humanoids. We do not
want to drift along dark
and deepless voids.

Erkut Tokman
Istanbul, Turkey

Vaccine, please make safe once more my most vulnerable loved ones. / Return their peace to them, they're the bravest people I know. / Please, vaccine, let us pass, we're halted on our journey and our dreams require us to cover some ground before nightfall. / Please, vaccine, let us rest, / breathing easy.

Shannon Rose McMaster
Youngstown, Ohio

'What about the risks?' / some ask, briskly. / To which I reply, friskily, / 'Life is risky!' / Seriously, the stats indicate / the jab's hazards / are specks of dust / placed on the scales / with a global wrecking ball – / in a choice between / millions more dead / and the promise of picnics . . . / I'm rolling up my sleeve / for a quick prick, / packing my hamper and mask / and filling my flask!

Naomi Foyle
Brighton, United Kingdom

We wake early and huddle around
the blue glow of the computer screen
just to add our names to the list,
never believing we'd be as excited
as kids on Christmas morning,
opening the gift of a needle that will
carry this hopeful medicine into us,
bringing relief to every set of red-
rimmed and weary eyes I see above
the masks. Inoculate me with the
kindness of a friend's hand on my
shoulder, my mother's yelp as she
sees it's me through the peephole,
then draws me safely into the circle
of her arms.

James Crews
Shaftsbury, Vermont

Dear Vaccine,

I will remember this winter of keeping vigil / You and I, illuminated / By a computer's glow // You were audacious, a beautiful obsession / I imagined you as a delicate thread / Each perfect amino acid / Shimmering // I watched winter through a window / Saw how the wind moves bare branches / Watched you enumerated and illustrated / Imagined / Shiny steel / Intricate diagrams / Analytical results // While you danced through my imagination / I felt my chest tighten / Edges pressed into me / Squares of faces / Calendar boxes / This black room // You became / Precious // I imagined you as points of light / Tracing shapes of highways / Across a dark globe // I hear / The cool edge of spring / A blackbird's return // Dear Vaccine, / May you stay fantastically cold / May you travel farther than I can imagine / May you set smiles free

Clara Ruth Kelly
Boxford, Massachusetts

Dear vaccine, from "vacca," your origin in cows, make us a herd. Be mother's milk to us now.

Katie Manning
San Diego, California

Dear vaccine, you give me hope /
Let me hug my friends, bump into
strangers / Let me travel the world
to see what I've missed / Let me
sweat and scream at a crowded
concert / Let me protect the lives
of those around me and those yet
to come / Let me expel a sigh of
relief / Let me say, 'I did my part'

Maria McGinnis
Stow, Ohio

The orange syringe. The thin syringe. The prick, the poke and the tears. What a joy!! Day after day, talking, smiling, cajoling and injecting my patients . . . my brethren . . . A humbling duty to serve, to protect and hold somebody's hand. Can we at last breathe a sigh of relief? Please promise me that I can . . . can't bear to see another paper with a grey heading . . . passed away . . . let it be COVID and not my patients!

Radhika Balu
London, United Kingdom

Dear vaccine, let me close
the distance, let me hold
my grandmother's hand,
and kiss the wrinkles on
her knuckles.

Caitie Young
Kent, Ohio

Dear vaccine, wrap your arms around me / As I offer mine, outstretched, grasping / Reaching for trust in your little glass vile / In your plunging medicine / I get your point.

Karen Green
Chatham, Ontario, Canada

It's the hugs we didn't know we loved. It's the class we didn't know we would miss. It's the smiles we didn't give enough. The things we never said, never did, and never will. It's the lives we thought would never end, jerking to a stop before our very eyes. Vaccine, will you save us? I thought I had time. We always think we have more time. Vaccine, please give us more time.

Hannah Hindman
Marana, Arizona

Dear vaccine,

You came along so fast /
we don't really know you
yet. But we want to love /
you. We need / you in us.

Joseph Ross
Washington, DC

Vaccine, keep me from kicking my own tires every morning when I wake up, to see if I'm still well.

Taddy McAllister
San Antonio, Texas

Vaccine, please let us sing / not just
in showers or alone in our cars / but
outside in parks, gardens, gazebos /
then inside schools, churches, cafes
/ in duos, trios, quartets and choirs /
Oh let all divas and crooners come out
/ out from the silence of quarantine
caves / chanters, rappers, throat
singers come / all yodelers and wild
ululators arise / a shot for together is
on the horizon / so raise your voices
in euphonious joy

Margot Lavoie
Portland, Oregon

Dear vaccine, you promise to end /
mother earth's longest gestation / of
hope, comfort and hugs. / Yes! a jab in
the arm brings relief; / anticipation
floods my soul. / Jubilance erupts and
breaks free / as children burst forth with
laughter; / running circles just for fun.
/ They chase, twirl, shriek with joy; /
dancing in the playground. / Then stop,
having spotted me, / my arms open, tears
streaming; / I wave and gesture them
over. / Yes! This will be the day, / I hug
my grandchildren again!

Jan Stretch
Victoria, British Columbia, Canada

Today your online portal surprised me with the message "book your appointment now." A wave of relief passed through my body, followed by this thought "maybe I can hold my new grandbaby Wyatt again soon." / I've been waiting around the edge of the vaccine dance floor for quite a while. Arms aching for the chance to hold him. / Thank you for asking me to dance!

Laura Wood
Owen Sound, Ontario, Canada

Dear vaccine, I'm counting on you to save another family from going through what we went through. I just wish you could have arrived a little sooner. I so hope everyone will get the vaccine as an act of charity that will serve the common good. Perhaps with more immunity, we will be able to lay my dad to rest and celebrate his life with our beloved family. Please get vaccinated. Our future is worth it.

Cindy Danes Bailey
Hilliard, Ohio

Last night I dreamed I got to put my hand right next to my granddaughter's tiny hand. Then my dear daughter in law whispered to me "You can hug her now. Go ahead." Not quite yet, but this will come true. Thanks to you.

Carolyn Fichter Galizio
Kent, Ohio

Vaccine, please,
free our senior
citizens to hug their
grandchildren and
take Silver Sneakers
classes together in
their retirement
homes, waving
their arms, gulping
in oxygen as they
march together.

Susan Kimball
Rochester, Minnesota

Dear vaccine . . . I'm a 1B grandma / I hunted and tracked you / hug hungry / smile starved / longing to sniff my son's newborn / needing to answer my daughter's 4 year old, Abbadabbers, sporting her unicorn mask / each day she'd ask, "Can we be close today, Nanny?" / "Soon" / stalking you at all hours / reboot redial reboot redial / then-Gotcha, you wonderful drive-through fast-food answer to the craving we all had come to accept / life resurrection in progress, dear Vaccine / today and tomorrow, leg hugs from Abbadabbers / today and tomorrow, I sniff the sweet breathe of a newborn. Love, 1B

Sally McGreevey Hannay
Comfort, Texas

Afterword

Throughout the COVID-19 pandemic, as lives were lost and routines were disrupted, Ohioans, like others throughout the world, looked forward to the day when they would be protected from the virus.

It was in those most difficult times when we found that we most needed poetry and other art forms to lift us with messages of hope and love. Creativity flourished. We saw children doing porch concerts for shut-in neighbors, chalk artists creating inspirational portraits on sidewalks, and people serenading one another from balconies and through nursing home windows.

Finally, the months of uncertainty, isolation, and anxiety gave way to hope with the arrival in December 2020 of the vaccine in Ohio. My wife, Fran, and I greeted some of the first vaccine delivery trucks in the Buckeye State. And, then, once we were eligible for our vaccines, we rolled up our sleeves during a live press conference to receive our shots—our tickets to family gatherings and hugs with our grandkids.

In the ensuing months, during our travels to vaccine clinics around the state, we found that many Ohioans shared our excitement about the vaccine. The promise of greater protection from COVID-19 brought with it the hope for brighter days ahead. Their collective sigh of relief, as well as the sorrow of loss, and the uncertainty of the time, are captured in the writings of *Dear Vaccine*.

Today, as the COVID-19 vaccine is widely available in Ohio, it is ushering in renewal and recovery in our state and many others, and creative industries are beginning to benefit.

Dear Vaccine offers a snapshot in time so that readers of the future can glimpse what it was like to anticipate and receive protection from a killer virus during a global pandemic.

We are grateful to the Ohio Arts Council, Kent State University, and the University of Arizona for supporting this project and other creative endeavors and applaud all those who foster and encourage the arts to preserve cultural heritage and strengthen our communities. We know the future is unpredictable, save for one certainty: We will all share the future, together. And that is all the more reason to rely on the arts, including *Dear Vaccine*, to learn more about ourselves and how we are all connected.

Mike DeWine
Governor of Ohio

Notes on the Contributors

Muna Agwa is a rising junior at Hathaway Brown School in Cleveland, Ohio. She enjoys reading and writing, swimming, problem-solving, and learning new things. She hopes that one day people can overcome their differences through art and empathy. Muna aspires to be a surgeon one day, although she hopes to never stop writing.

Denise Alden lives and writes in the Twin Cities in Minnesota. She's worked in healthcare and owned a small business, and now she cares for her family and her writing. She especially loves and is grateful for the poetry of Jericho Brown and Derrick Austin. Some of her work can be found at *Scalawag Magazine* and *Holy Flea Dream Journal.*

Lahab Assef Al-Jundi lives in San Antonio, Texas, and his poetry has appeared in collections such as *In These Latitudes, Ten Contemporary Poets,* and *Inclined to Speak: An Anthology of Arab American Poetry,* as well as many other anthologies and literary journals. His latest poetry collection, *No Faith at All,* was published by Pecan Grove Press. A new collection is forthcoming in early 2022 from Kelsay Books titled *This Is It.*

Lynda Allen considers herself a life in progress and a listener. She lives with her husband in Fredericksburg, Virginia, where she writes poetry and fiction, paints, makes jewelry, and communes with her beloved

Rappahannock River. During the pandemic, the natural world has been a saving grace for Lynda, where she found she could embrace nature and all its beauty even if she couldn't embrace her human friends.

As a high school English teacher, Arizona resident **Teresa Anthofer** tells her students that our writing makes us vulnerable—and because that vulnerability reveals our true selves and creates something meaningful, Teresa enjoys writing alongside her students. In addition to iambic pentameter lessons that involve intense gestures, Teresa celebrates poetry in the classroom with the weekly tradition of Haikusday. She and her husband enjoy dining at Indian restaurants and supporting local theatre, activities they plan to do much more of once their young children are able to get vaccinated. Two of her favorite words are juxtapose and discombobulate, and she has resolved to never again use the word unprecedented.

Samantha Antoine is a two-time alum of Kent State University. She currently works at the University of Michigan in an international and multigenerational community of graduate students and their families. She is passionate about access and equity in higher education. Samantha lives in Ann Arbor with her family.

Cindy Danes Bailey is a retired RN living in Hilliard, Ohio. She worked in family practice, a nursing home facility, and in a sheltered workshop for adults with developmental disabilities. Presently she is on standby for anything her children or grandchildren need.

Dr. **Radhika Balu** is a general practitioner who lives and works in Harrow, London. She has worked as a family medicine practitioner for 15 years. During the pandemic, she has primarily worked in the COVID-19 hub and vaccination centers. She believes that art plays a vital role in healing and poetry captures the emotions of a soul—the anguish, joy, and relief. She enjoys trekking, dancing, and spending time with her family.

Kami Bates (she/her/hers) is from Olympia, Washington, majored in English at Pepperdine University, and has lived in Tucson, Arizona, since April 2020. She studies speech language pathology at the University of Arizona and will graduate with her master's degree in May 2022. She has two "pandemic pets," a pit bull–husky mix named Misty and a black cat called Jiji. The best part of the pandemic has been getting to spend so much time with Kersti, her amazing fiancée, and they can't wait to get married in June 2022! Kami loves writing, the Enneagram, staying hydrated, dancing, watching TV with subtitles, and being queer.

Dorothy Beavington lives in Surrey, British Columbia, Canada. She is a retired social worker and journalist who enjoys dancing and reading. Her greatest accomplishments were raising four amazing sons and raising over $50,000 at her birthday parties for children and famine relief in developing countries. She fell in love with poetry as a child, and her son, Lee, is a respected poet who is working on his first poetry book. Dorothy survived the pandemic by the side of her sweet and funny husband, Robert, who cracked her up daily with his humor and kept her sane.

Linda C. Belans is a poet, dancer, and author of *States of Being: Leadership Coaching for Equitable Schools*. She was first awakened to poetry about 30 years ago when her friend Shirley handed her a copy of *Words Under the Words* by Naomi Shihab Nye. Linda lives in Durham, North Carolina, where she grandparents six children with her partner, Jim Lee.

Margo Berdeshevsky lives in Paris, France. Her latest collection, *Before the Drought* (Glass Lyre Press), was a finalist for the National Poetry Series. She has two books forthcoming: *It Is Still Beautiful to Hear the Heart Beat* (Salmon Poetry, in Ireland) and *Kneel Said the Night (A Hybrid Book in Half-Notes)* (Sundress Publications). She is also the author of *Between Soul & Stone, But a Passage in Wilderness* (Sheep Meadow Press) and *Beautiful Soon Enough*, recipient of FC2's Ronald Sukenick Innovative Fiction Award. Her love for poetry began in a first career in New York theater. She later lived in the Hawaiian Islands at the edge of the rainforest for 20 years and taught there as a poet in the schools. Pandemic life forced an embrace of solitude and silences the poet requires but may lose en route to publication. For more information, please visit http://margoberdeshevsky.com.

Vivian Blatnik was adopted in China as a baby and raised in Kent, Ohio. She is a sophomore at Theodore Roosevelt High School in Kent. She enjoys spending time with her family and pets. She is open to trying new things, most recently karate, whitewater rafting, and softball. She has been involved in the visual arts in Art in the Park, a citywide arts festival, taking first place twice in the youth competition. This is her first published poem.

Sally Bliumis-Dunn teaches modern poetry at Manhattanville College and the Palm Beach Poetry Festival. Her third full-length collection, *Echolocation*, published by Plume Editions/Madhat Press in March 2018, was on the long list for the Julie Suk Award and a finalist for the Eric Hoffer Award. In 2002, she was a finalist for the Nimrod and Hardman's Pablo Neruda Prize. She just became a grandmother and lives in Armonk, New York.

David J. Bodney has practiced media and constitutional law, based in Phoenix, Arizona, for over 40 years. For most of that time, he has taught media law as adjunct faculty at Arizona State University. He briefly served as a newspaper editor, where he wrote a weekly column. Married with three grown children, David is a member of the Upaya Zen Center, which awakened a love of haiku. In his professional life, he fights for open government and First Amendment freedoms.

Marie Boucher is an English professor at the Middlebury Institute of International Studies in Monterey, California, who organizes an annual Poetry Week at the institute and contributes regularly to literary journals, open mics, and Wednesday Night Poetry. She has recently enjoyed workshops with Danusha Laméris, Naomi Shihab Nye, and Nickole Brown. She loves spending time with trees, conducting watershed education, and composing poetry during these ongoing pandemic times.

Bill Bradley Senator William W. Bradley, 78, is a managing director of Allen & Company LLC. From 2001 to 2004, he acted as chief outside advisor to McKinsey & Company's nonprofit practice. He was a senior advisor and vice chairman of the International Council of JP Morgan & Co., Inc., from 1997 to 1999. During that time, he also worked as an essayist for CBS Evening News and was a visiting professor at Stanford University, University of Notre Dame, and the University of Maryland. Senator Bradley served in the US Senate from 1979 to 1997 representing the state of New Jersey. In 2000, he was a candidate for the Democratic nomination for President of the United States. Prior to serving in the

Senate, he was an Olympic gold medalist in 1964 and a professional basketball player with the New York Knicks from 1967 to 1977, during which time they won two NBA championships. In 1982, he was elected to the Basketball Hall of Fame. Senator Bradley holds a BA degree in American history from Princeton University and an MA degree from Oxford University where he was a Rhodes Scholar. He has authored seven books on American politics, culture, and economy, including his latest book, *We Can All Do Better*. Currently, Senator Bradley hosts *American Voices*, a weekly show on Sirius XM Satellite Radio that highlights the remarkable accomplishments of Americans both famous and unknown. He currently lives in New York City, New York.

Jenny Browne was the 2017–18 Poet Laureate of Texas. She lives in downtown San Antonio and teaches at Trinity University. She grows beans and drinks coffee. She spent much of the pandemic taking long walks with her now quite large COVID-19 puppy, a spotted Texas heeler mutt named Belfast.

Jade Busca is a young woman who lives in Marseille, France, with her fiancée. She is in her fourth year of medical studies and dreams to become a pediatric surgeon. She is also very attracted by social sciences and medical ethics, and she recently obtained a master's degree combining these fields. She has always been interested in poetry and wrote tiny poems in her diary when she was a little girl. This is her first published poem.

Sophia Caparisos is a retired English teacher living in Savannah, Georgia, whose love of reading poetry is surpassed only by discussing or teaching it. After watching her spend half a lifetime (part of every day for 34 years) sitting at the kitchen table grading papers and annotating texts, Sophia's daughter opted to become a teacher, too. Sophia considers this an important tribute to the profession and a boon to future students. These days, Sophia's favorite future students are her three preschool grandchildren.

Mary Ellen Chown is an educator living in Oakville, Ontario, and is the mother of three grown children. She has been a feminist advocate for change in the Catholic Church for over 20 years. She loves to gather round a table with family and friends and to enjoy the gifts of the seasons: a hike in autumn's color, cross country skiing in a winter forest, tending perennials in spring, and jumping into a brisk summer lake. Poetry is the place she goes to pause and reflect. Her first collection of poetry and art, *grace drifts in*, was published in December 2021.

Sonnet Kekilia Coggins lives on the island of Maui, Hawaii, with her husband and two young sons. She directs the Merwin Conservancy, which furthers the legacy of poet, ecologist, and activist W. S. Merwin. During the pandemic, she was grateful for the invitation, disguised though it was, to feel the pulse, rhythms, and cries of her island home.

Brendan Constantine is a poet based in Los Angeles, California. His work has appeared in many of the nation's standards, including *Poetry*, *Tin House*, *Best American Poetry*, *Poetry Daily*, and *Poem-a-Day*. A popular performer, Brendan has presented his work to audiences throughout the United States and Europe, also appearing on NPR's All Things Considered, TED ED, numerous podcasts, and YouTube. He currently teaches at the Windward School and, since 2017, has been developing poetry workshops for people with aphasia.

Fabio Corsini, PhD, is professor and coordinator of the CCI Communication Program at Kent State University Florence Center. He lives in Rome, teaching different communication and media classes. When he is not in class, he is probably watching a movie or an episode of a TV show. He likes poetry and its capability of empowering people and bringing beauty and meaning into people's lives.

James Crews is a poet and editor living with his husband in Shaftsbury, Vermont. He has taught creative writing for over 15 years and has edited several anthologies including *How to Love the World: Poems of Gratitude and Hope*. Coffee, long hikes, and keeping a daily kindness journal have helped him to survive the pandemic.

Marc A. Crowley is a retired teacher who lives in Cochise County in rural southeastern Arizona. He taught American History and Government and was the founder of the Mock Trial Program at the high school where he taught. He has traveled extensively in the western United States, and his poetry has been about life's transitions, spirituality, and his environment from oceans to the borderlands where he now lives. He has been writing poetry since 1968 and has had a few poems published over the years. He is currently compiling his first book of poetry.

Alison Hawthorne Deming is a poet and essayist who lives in Tucson, Arizona, and Grand Manan Island, New Brunswick, Canada. She is professor emerita at the University of Arizona. Her most recent book is *A Woven World*. She is the author of five poetry collections with a new book, *The Excavations*, near completion. She likes to garden, play piano, and play with her goldendoodle.

Sean Parker Dennison is a painter, poet, partner, parent, and Unitarian Universalist minister who lives in Medford, Oregon.

Todd Diacon lives in Kent, Ohio, and serves as president of Kent State University. He is a firm believer in the power of poetry to explore the human condition. As a child he watched his father, a small-town physician, participate in polio vaccination events, and he appreciates all that is being done to keep people safe during the COVID-19 pandemic.

Joanne Feenstra lives with her amazing partner and two more-or-less-amazing-most-of-the-time dogs, in very rural British Columbia, Canada, where, after a career of working with marginalized individuals in suburban British Columbia, Joanne and her partner followed their amazing children and grandchildren and moved to the West Kootenays. She is learning to be retired, to let go of things that don't bring joy or peace or gratefulness. She is learning to be doglike and "chase sticks" instead of folding socks.

Silke Feltz is an assistant teaching professor who teaches English composition at the University of Oklahoma. Originally from Germany and now residing in Norman, Oklahoma, Silke enjoys writing poetry and directs StreetKnits, a humanitarian knitting charity that knits for the unhoused. Life has been challenging for everybody during the pandemic, and poetry gives her hope that we will eventually find our way back to one another.

Meg Files is a retired community college teacher in Tucson, Arizona. She is the author of several books of fiction and poetry as well as a book about taking risks in writing. She directs the Tucson Festival of Books

Masters Workshop. During the pandemic, she has taught virtual writing workshops and classes and read more books than ever. One day, she might once again enjoy scuba diving.

Naomi Foyle is a British-Canadian writer, educator, and activist. The author of three poetry collections and five science fiction novels, including the eco-SF quartet *The Gaia Chronicles*, she lives in Brighton, United Kingdom, and teaches creative writing at the University of Chichester. She enjoys wild swimming, hiking, cycling, photography, traveling, and exercising her right to protest. A supporter of a just peace in Israel-Palestine, she has visited the Middle East often, volunteering on eco-projects and hosting poetry readings. She has read her own work in the United Kingdom, Europe, North America, South Korea, and Iraq.

Candace Frede lives in the West Village of Manhattan, New York. She has been drawn to poetry since childhood. She recently retired from a career in digital design and information technology. During quarantine, the outlines of life were a small apartment with two cats and a neighborhood with a temporary morgue. The Hudson River Promenade on a good day—a day without crowds—was one place to breathe fresh air mask-free. A treasured community spot was closed. Her poem here is about that place.

Carolyn Fichter Galizio is a retired teacher from the Kent State University Child Development Center. She grew up in Kent, Ohio, and she and her husband Kim have two adult sons, two daughters-in-law, and five wonderful grandchildren they adore. She loves her family, friends, literature, music, nature, animals, and believes in fighting for human rights.

When **Catherine Elizabeth Gamblin** turned 67, she thought it was time to write. She does not have an MFA, but she has hovered near brilliant writers, listening, reading, waiting. She has self-published three zines that merge with her art education: drawing with words. During the pandemic, she was told she had an abnormal mammogram, but surgery found no cancer. Her poetry and drawings have tethered her to her body. She lives in Otis, Oregon.

Emily Gammons is an archivist in Tucson, Arizona, and a recent graduate of the University of Arizona, where they earned the second half of their master's degree through Zoom. Originally from Columbus, Ohio, their favorite poets include Ada Limón, E. E. Cummings, and Edna St. Vincent Millay. When the pandemic is over, they hope to join a choir again. This is their first published poem; they thank you for reading it and wish you health, strength, and good fortune.

Dawn Garisch finds poems in difficult situations and on mountain hikes in her home of Cape Town, South Africa. She is a medical doctor and founding member of an NPO, the Life Righting Collective (https://www.liferighting.com/), teaching poetry and life writing as a resource for mental health. Both reading and writing poetry have been an anchor in her life during times of great stress, including during the pandemic. She has had seven novels, two collections of poetry, a nonfiction work, and a memoir published. Her second collection of poetry, *Disturbance* (Karavan Press), came out in 2020.

Joan Beth Gerstein, originally from New York, has resided in Oceanside, California, since 1969. A retired educator and psychotherapist, Joan taught creative writing to incarcerated veterans for five years until the pandemic. Her first book of poetry, *Theories of Relativity*, was just published this month by Garden Oak Press. Joan's poetry has appeared in more than 30 anthologies, journals and online zines.

Dr. **Shihab M. A. Ghanem** is a father of three and a grandfather of six, all currently living in Dubai, United Arab Emirates. He is a retired engineer who worked for 40 years as the plant manager of Gulf Eternit, then director of engineering of Dubai Ports and Jebel Ali Free Zone, then managing director of Mohammad bin Rashed Technology Park. He has published 90 books in Arabic and English, 20 of which are books of verse. He has received about 30 awards, mostly for poetry or translation of poetry, including the Tagore Peace Award and an honorary doctorate from Soka University in Japan. During the pandemic he has been able to publish with the WhatsApp group of 90 Arab poets and intellectuals that he formed. Please visit www.shihabghanem.com.

Elizabeth Gillespie is a grandmother who lives in London, Ontario. She is a retired nurse who worked in several different settings including hospital ICUs and visiting home nursing. During the pandemic, she has come to appreciate many little things close to home. It turns out her bookshelves are full of interesting old treasures, including poetry.

Aleksandra Golos grew up in Vancouver, Canada, and currently lives in Philadelphia, Pennsylvania. Since graduating from the Wharton School at the University of Pennsylvania, she has conducted research at the intersection of behavioral science, social listening, and COVID-19. Aleksandra lives with Type 1 diabetes and aspires to become a physician, with the goal of caring for others with chronic illnesses. She firmly believes in the healing power of poetry; amid the uncertainty of pandemic life, it helps her find comfort in the everyday certainties that remain. This is her first published poem.

Amoaba Gooden, PhD, serves as the vice president for the Division of Diversity, Equity, and Inclusion at Kent State University where she is also a professor of Africana Studies. For over 20 years, Amoaba Gooden has conducted equity, diversity, and inclusion work with colleges and universities, K-12 schools, and organizations across North America. She lives in Kent, Ohio, enjoys learning about different spiritual practices, and loves reading and working with healing herbs. This is her second published poem.

Liz Gray has been writing poetry since middle school. She has also written a memoir, professional articles, many book reviews, and hundreds of social media posts. She was an English teacher and librarian at high schools in Italy, England, Switzerland, and Massachusetts for 37 years. Today Liz spends her time quilting, knitting, traveling, and reorganizing the contents of her home in Newton, Massachusetts.

Karen Green is a freelance writer in Chatham, Ontario, where she lives with her family and "pandemic puppy." Her poetry has appeared in many print and online publications, and she is grateful to have the opportunity to help transcribe this moment in history.

Mary Zettelman Greer lives in Shalersville, Ohio. She is a retired teacher. She has been writing poetry since 1965 and has published four volumes of poetry. She was a grateful student and friend of Kent's beloved poet Maj Ragain, and she enjoys participating in Kent's monthly poetry readings and gatherings.

Bruce Gungle lives on the west side of Tucson, Arizona. After studying creative writing and atmospheric science, he wound up with a job as a hydrologist with the USGS for the past 22 years. He spends his free time running ridiculously long distances, mountain biking, growing adeniums, and hiking with his black and tan coonhound Flatt McCurb. To bring perspective and context to this surreal time, Bruce has been writing a four-line poem each day of this pandemic year, 2021.

Sarah Gzemski is a poet living and working in Tucson, Arizona. She is the marketing specialist at the University of Arizona Poetry Center and the managing editor of Noemi Press.

Sally McGreevey Hannay is a wife, mother, grandmother, teacher, and weekend poet from Comfort, Texas. She earned her MFA in creative writing from the University of Iowa Writers' Workshop and taught college writing for 40 years. She recently retired from Schreiner University as a professor of English and has published poems as the recipient of the Conference for College Teachers of English prize for original poetry in 2012 and 2014 and in *The Texas Observer*. Her collection of poems, *They Aren't Your Ducks,* was published in 2020 by Resource Publishing. She loves family, friends, camping, hiking, and yoga.

Julie Heifetz, originally from Maryland, is currently living in San Miguel de Allende, Mexico. She is the author of poems in anthologies and three nonfiction books, the latest of which is *As Far As the I Can See,* a memoir. Poetry makes her remember who she is. The pandemic intensified her need to reach others through her words.

Before retirement and COVID-19 quarantine, **Fran Hillyer** taught upper school English at the Episcopal School of Dallas for almost 30 years. During that time, she earned a PhD in humanities from the University of Texas at Dallas. She also has an MA in English from Bowling Green

State University and a BA in psychology from DePaul University. In 2018, she also received an MFA in creative writing from Queens University in Charlotte, North Carolina. Now she lives in Glorieta, New Mexico. She has recently completed her first novel.

Hannah Hindman is a student from Tucson, Arizona. She is highly involved in athletics, clubs, and academics. She enjoys reading novels and poetry. She also likes running, tennis, and being outside. This is her first published poem.

Eleni Hines was born and raised in southern New Brunswick, Canada, a place that is permeated with the salty tang of the ocean just out of sight. A place of trees and shadows. A place filled with kind people and (sometimes) unhurried days. She currently works as a laboratory technician but also spends her days painting and making and dreaming. She enjoys being curious and seeking out new experiences and stories, and she has always found solace and connection with the world though poetry, both written and through writing. The pandemic has been long and may yet be longer. She has experienced love and loss during this time. The former is a glowing, lovely thing. The latter has redefined her. She wishes you wellness and wants to let you know that she loves you.

Tish Hinojosa is a Mexican American singer songwriter born in San Antonio, Texas, and living most recently in Austin, Texas. She is the youngest of 13 children born to two Mexican immigrants who, as stated in her song, "The West Side of Town," "made a good life, the hard way." Her songs blend the genres of country, folk and Hispanic music in a way that can only be described as a musical melting pot: unique and insightful. She sings and writes in Spanish and English and has many bilingual songs, including a full album of children's songs that has often been used by teachers as a tool for teaching the Spanish language.

Elizabyth A. Hiscox lives in Fort Collins, Colorado. She is the author of *Reassurance in Negative Space* (Word Galaxy, 2017). She has taught writing in England, the Czech Republic, Spain, and the United States During the pandemic she has learned to grow Sweet 100s and Straight Eights (tomatoes and cucumbers, respectively).

Isaiah Hunt is an Ohio-born writer and teacher who enjoys nothing more than sharing his obsession toward storytelling with others. He is a third-year student at the Northeast Ohio Masters of Fine Arts Program. He lives in Cleveland and enjoys long drives, being with family, and daydreaming about worlds adjacent to our own.

Tanya Huntington is a binational writer, artist, actor, and traveler based in Mexico City, Mexico. Her most prolific work as an illustrator, *Vidas sin fronteras*, features 50 portraits of people who abandoned their home country and changed the world, as a celebration of migrants and their contributions to humanity. Her most recent book of poetry, *Solastalgia*, expresses the need for poets to find a way to reconnect with nature despite environmental devastation. During the pandemic, she loved playing gin rummy every night with her husband and drawing pictures with her son, even though she hated staying put.

Luisa A. Igloria teaches in the MFA Creative Writing Program at Old Dominion University and at the nonprofit Muse Writing Center in her home of Norfolk, Virginia—mostly by Zoom during the last 18+ months of the pandemic. In 2020, she was appointed the 20th Poet Laureate of the Commonwealth of Virginia. When she isn't writing or teaching, she enjoys hand binding books, knitting, cooking, and baking. For more information, please visit www.luisaigloria.com.

Julie Swarstad Johnson is a poet who lives in Tucson, Arizona, where she works as the Archivist & Outreach Librarian at the University of Arizona Poetry Center. She is the author of the poetry collection *Pennsylvania Furnace* (Unicorn Press, 2019) and the chapbook *Orchard Light* (Seven Kitchens Press, 2020); she also coedited the anthology *Beyond Earth's Edge: The Poetry of Spaceflight* (University of Arizona Press, 2020). While working at home during the pandemic, Julie learned how to produce a podcast for the Poetry Center from her living room—look for *Poetry Centered* on your favorite podcast platform.

Jessica Jones (MA, University of Montana) is full-time faculty at Kent State University at Stark, where she teaches poetry, Native American literature, and composition courses that focus on social justice. She also regularly teaches tribal youth in Indian Country, Montana. She enjoys time with friends and family and being in the woods. Her book *Bitterroot* (2018) can be found at Finishing Line Press.

Rivka Joseph is a mother of one who lives in Cleveland, Ohio. She attended Kent State University and is an MSW student at Case Western Reserve University. She is currently working at University Hospitals with pediatric victims of peer and community violence. She has previously worked with victims of child sexual abuse as an advocate. Rivka enjoys spending time with her son and photographing nature. She completed her first year of graduate school during the pandemic, as well as being in the field working with children. Rivka has used poetry as a journaling technique for many years; however, this is her first published poem.

Dean R. Kahler is a retired public servant who lives in Canton, Ohio. He enjoys distance running.

Peter Kahn is a poet-educator based in Chicago, Illinois. A founding member of London-based Malika's Poetry Kitchen, he has been teaching in Oak Park, Illinois, since 1994, with two stints living/teaching in London. He writes to be a good role model for his students. Peter is the coeditor of *The Golden Shovel Anthology: New Poems Honoring Gwendolyn Brooks* and *Respect the Mic: Celebrating 20 Years of Poetry from a Chicagoland High School*. He wants immersive poetry programming to thrive in all schools and works to promote student voice.

Erin Kearney, originally from Nova Scotia, is now a lawyer in Ontario. During Canada's initial COVID-19 waves, Erin lived with family in southern Ontario while her fiancée worked the frontlines of the deadliest long-term care home outbreak in the province's Northwest. The two are now married and expecting their first child in the spring of 2022. Her first published nonacademic work, this poem is dedicated to Erin's late grandmother, Barbara Minaker, a prolific poet.

Clara Ruth Kelly spent the fall and winter of 2020 to 2021 working to start up a manufacturing suite dedicated to production of the Pfizer-BioNTech COVID-19 vaccine. She and husband Patrick spent much of the pandemic working in makeshift home offices amid piles of LEGOs and laundry while striving to keep their two sons fed, diapered, and content. The best days of lockdown included walking or cycling on trails near their home in Boxford, Massachusetts. Other pandemic joys were picking fruit and reading picture books. She read Naomi Shihab Nye's book *Fuel* to her four-year-old son, Orion, while backyard camping in May 2020. Her two-year-old son Rigel's pandemic poem of June 2021 was "Hooray, Strawberries!"

C. Louise Kennedy is the Executive Director of the Laura (Riding) Jackson Foundation in Vero Beach, Florida. She is an educator most proud of the educational and humanitarian work she has done in Kenya and at Saint Edward's School in Vero Beach. She loves creating programs that bring students together, and she has a strong belief in the power of words to heal. As part of her navigation through the pandemic, she spent time developing a spiritual practice around writing haiku so that she could stay engaged in nature.

Stuart Kestenbaum lives in Deer Isle, Maine. He is the author of six collections of poems, most recently *Things Seemed to Be Breaking* (Deerbrook Editions, 2021) and a collection of essays, *The View from Here* (Brynmorgen Press). He was the host of the Maine Public Radio program *Poems from Here* and the host/curator of the podcasts *Make/Time* and *Voices of the Future*. He served as Maine's Poet Laureate from 2016 to 2021. For many years he was the director of the Haystack Mountain School of Crafts. During the pandemic he spent as much time as he could walking, cross-country skiing, or ice skating.

Suzanne Kilkus is a retired marriage and family therapist, working for over 35 years and living in Madison, Wisconsin. She is happily married, a mother of three, and a grandmother of four delightful human beings. Meditation and teaching are a primary part of her life. She's dedicated to embodied and warmhearted actions for racial and social justice. She enjoys family and friend gatherings, walking, qigong, reading, and living. This is her first published poem.

Susan Kimball is a retired high school language arts teacher living in Rochester, Minnesota. She taught five years in Guttenberg, Iowa, and 30 years at Cedar Falls High School in Cedar Falls, Iowa. In 2002, Susan was granted a Fulbright Memorial Fellowship to study the Japanese educational system for three weeks, along with 200 other American teachers. Susan enjoys the practices of journal keeping and T'ai Chi Chih. Reading poetry and participating in the online Poetry of Resilience sessions provided nourishment and hope during COVID-19 isolation.

Taylor Kirby is a writer who lives in Austin, Texas. She works at a non-profit that connects low-income adults with free college courses in the humanities. Her time is spent with her partner, her rescue pets (two cats and a greyhound), and her collection of pandemic houseplants.

Alvena Gael Kirkpatrick lives in Ojai, California, and is a mindfulness and compassion educator with UCLA's Mindful Awareness Research Center. Her graduate degree is in mythology and depth psychology. She is the author of *Roam: Ojai's Hip Little Hiking Guide* and is the editor of many books. She is also published in the anthology *She Is Everywhere*, which highlights women's feminist and environmental writing. Her passions are watersheds, wolves, and mythopoetics.

Denise Kitagawa lives in Alberta, Canada, where she enjoys hiking, cycling, kayaking, and nature photography with family and friends. A longtime advocate for a daily dose of nature, she is editor in chief at geoks.ca, where she writes with the goal of inspiring others to head outside. Her best investment during the pandemic has been a countertop pizza oven! This is her second published poem.

Yahia Lababidi, a Lebanese-Egyptian poet based in the United States, is the author of nine books. Lababidi has been called "our greatest living aphorist," and his prose/poetry meditations have gone viral, are used in classrooms and religious services, and have been featured in international film festivals. Lababidi has also contributed to literary and cultural institutions throughout the United States, Europe and the Middle East, such as: Oxford University, Pearson, PBS NewsHour, NPR and HBO. Lababidi views the global pandemic as a period of enforced mass meditation reminding us of our inescapable interdependence. Lababidi's publications during this critical moment in our lives include *Revolutions of the Heart* (Wipf and Stock, 2020), a book of essays and conversations exploring crises and transformation, as well as *Learning to Pray* (Kelsay Books, 2021), a collection of his new and selected spiritual aphorisms and poems.

Paula J. Lambert has authored several collections of poetry including *The Ghost of Every Feathered Thing* (FutureCycle, 2022) and *How to See the World* (Bottom Dog, 2020), a 2021 Ohioana Book Awards finalist. A literary and visual artist, Lambert lives in Columbus, Ohio, with her husband Dr. Michael Perkins, a philosopher and technologist.

Danusha Laméris is a poet and essayist who lives in a barn in Santa Cruz, California. She's the author of *Bonfire Opera*, which won the 2021 Northern California Book Award in Poetry, and spends her spare time walking through the redwoods and planting for pollinators.

Margot Lavoie's poetry has appeared in *Natural Bridge*, *Northeast Corridor*, *Poesia*, *Red Owl*, and the *Seasons*. A native of Syracuse, New York, Margot has lived in Arkansas, Pennsylvania, Wisconsin, and, briefly, in Oklahoma. Currently she lives in Portland, Oregon, with her husband Tom. She earns her living working as a medical records coder. She lives through writing, music, her garden, her grandsons, and the support of a wonderful circle of family and friends.

Genevieve Lehr is an award-winning poet who lives in Nova Scotia, Canada. She is the author of several books of poetry, and her work has been published in a variety of literary journals both in Canada and abroad. She's passionate about the funky kingdom of fungi, forages in the wild, gardens with friends, and rescues injured birds who find her. She despairs over the pandemic of ignorance and wonkiness fueled by social media. She is often silent. And calm.

Brenda Liddy lives in Belfast, Northern Ireland. She was an English teacher in a college and teaches a creative writing class at Queen's University. She has published a few books and has had a few poems published in local anthologies. She practices mindfulness and attends yoga classes. She has always enjoyed reading poetry, and one of her favorite poets is Seamus Heaney. During lockdown she learned how to teach online by using Zoom, and she learned to live more mindfully.

Born in New York City, **Carl Little** has lived in Somesville, Maine, on Mount Desert Island since 1989. He holds degrees from Dartmouth (BA), Middlebury (MA), and Columbia (MFA). Little is the author of

Ocean Drinker: New & Selected Poems. He recently retired from the Maine Community Foundation after 20 years managing communications. In 2021, the Dorothea and Leo Rabkin Foundation awarded Little a Lifetime Achievement Award for his art writing.

Jodi Lundgren lives on the traditional territory of the Lekwungen and W̱SÁNEĆ peoples on Canada's west coast. She has published a literary novel, *Touched*, as well as titles for young adults, including *Leap and Blow*. She is on the faculty at Thompson Rivers University (Open Learning), where she teaches literature and writing. The stillness of the pandemic reignited her interest in both poetry and growing food. In 2021, an ailing pear tree in her yard produced an unexpected crop, and she baked her first-ever homegrown crisp.

Former Kentucky Poet Laureate **George Ella Lyon** writes in multiple genres for readers of all ages. Her recent poetry collections include *Back to the Light* and *Many-Storied House* (University Press of Kentucky, 2013 and 2021), as well as *Voices of Justice: Poems about People Working for a Better World* (Holt Books for Young Readers, 2020). Lyon's poem "Where I'm From" has gone around the world as a writing model. During the lockdown, she wrote, read, prayed, gardened, and taught Zoom workshops. A mother and grandmother, Lyon works as a freelance writer and teacher based in Lexington, Kentucky. For additional information, please visit www.georgeellalyon.com.

Lindsay Mann is a first-grade teacher in Ann Arbor, Michigan. She has been working as an educator for the past 16 years and received her doctorate in curriculum and teaching at Teachers College, Columbia University in May 2019, with a focus on early literacy. She has also taught literacy courses at Teachers College and the University of Michigan. Lindsay enjoys writing and working alongside all learners big and small and has continued to teach first graders and graduate students throughout the pandemic remotely and in person. She continues to lean on poetry, her daily walks, and the people who she meets along the way for inspiration. She is honored to be a part of the *Dear Vaccine* poetry anthology.

Katie Manning is the founding editor in chief of *Whale Road Review* and a professor of writing at Point Loma Nazarene University in San Diego,

California. She is the author of *Tasty Other*, which won the 2016 Main Street Rag Poetry Book Award, and five chapbooks. Her poem, "What to Expect," was recently featured on the Poetry Unbound podcast from the On Being Project. She enjoys baking, beaches, books, board games, and alliteration.

Susan Markovich, a newly retired psychiatric nursing faculty member of the University of Arizona, is investing her time in taking Humanities Seminar classes, serving on fine arts boards of directors, and "Floating with Friends" (aqua-aeorobics)! She loves all the performing arts—singing, dancing, theatre—as well as sports, finance, and politics. What has been most fun? Visiting sons and grandsons in the Bay Area. Now she is a published poet. What a pleasant surprise! She splits her time between Waterloo, Iowa and Tucson, Arizona.

Taddy McAllister is a retired bureaucrat, entrepreneur, and school-teacher who has written four books: *Wander Lust*, *Fugitive Pieces*, *Rut*, and *Beezie*. She lives in San Antonio, Texas, and raises money for her various causes.

Tina McGill is a 63-year-old recently relocated to Ontario, Canada. She worked with her husband and son for 20 years providing prosthetics and custom bracing devices in Hawaii. When she and her husband retired, they drove across the United States from Seattle, Washington, to Ontario, Canada. The experience of driving cross country during the early days of the pandemic was her inspiration to journal and write poetry. She is a hospice volunteer and wishes peace and love to all.

Maria McGinnis is a May 2021 Kent State graduate who lives in northeast Ohio. She currently works as a freelance journalist, writing for both local and larger national publications. She loves writing of any kind and has always enjoyed poetry. When she's not writing, she likes spending time with her friends and family, hiking, and baking.

Shannon Rose McMaster is a recent graduate from Kent State, where she studied anthropology and art history. She currently works at Youngstown State University in Youngstown, Ohio, where she helps to develop overseas programs. Shannon enjoys trying new recipes and visiting as many museums as she can. Her love of poetry took off when she was hired as a student assistant at the Wick Poetry Center in 2020. Poetry found her when she needed it most and continues to be a part of her life.

Minnesota writer and teacher **Bill Meissner** is the author of ten books. His newest collection, a book of short stories with a baseball theme, is *Light at the Edge of the Field* (Stephen F. Austin University Press). He has published five collections of poetry. His latest is *The Mapmaker's Dream* (Finishing Line Press). Bill's novel, *Spirits in the Grass* (University of Notre Dame Press), won the Midwest Book Award. His two books of short stories are *Hitting into the Wind* and *The Road to Cosmos*. His forthcoming book, which features grassroots baseball photography and poetic prose, is *Circling toward Home* (Finishing Line Press). Bill's hobbies and interests include travel, rock music, baseball, photography, pulp fiction magazines, and collecting vintage typewriters. He lives in St. Cloud with his wife, Christine. His Facebook author page is https://www.facebook.com/wjmeissner/.

Philip Metres of University Heights, Ohio, has written numerous books including *Shrapnel Maps*. Awarded fellowships from the Guggenheim and Lannan Foundations, as well as three Arab American Book Awards, he is professor of English and director of the Peace, Justice, and Human Rights Program at John Carroll University, and faculty at Vermont College of Fine Arts' MFA program.

Melanie Miller is a retired school librarian and yoga teacher who lives in Columbus, Ohio. She spends her time caring for her family and her spunky wire fox terrier, Henry. In seventh grade she won a poetry contest with her recitation of Robert Frost's "Looking for a Sunset Bird in Winter." This is her first published poem.

Kate McCarroll Moore served as the Poet Laureate for the City of San Ramon, California for three consecutive terms between 2012 and 2018, and she believes in the power of poetry to build empathy and transform lives. She's the author of *Avians of Mourning*, a poetry chapbook, and *Alphapoetica: A Poetry Primer for the Everyday Poet*. Kate is also the author of two novels for children. From her home in Danville, California, she teaches online writing courses and serves as a book coach for a nonprofit organization that connects low-income families with access to high quality books.

Majid Naficy was considered the Arthur Rimbaud of Persian poetry. He fled Iran a year and half after his wife Ezzat was executed in Evin Prison, Tehran. He received his doctorate at UCLA in 1996 and lives in Los Angeles, California, with his son Azad.

Julie Naslund—mother, partner, gardener, poet—lives and writes in the high desert of Bend, Oregon. She feels that writing poetry is an act of translation. Her work has been published in various print and online publications.

Robbi Nester of Lake Forest, California, is a poet and retired college educator who has spent the pandemic hosting and attending generative poetry workshops and readings. Though the scope of her physical travel has been limited by the virus, she has probably met more people and explored more topics during this time than ever before. Robbi is the author of four books of poetry and editor of three anthologies. Her website may be found at https://www.robbinester.net/.

Carrie Newcomer is songwriter, performing artist, author, and activist. She has 19 albums including *Until Now* and *The Beautiful Not Yet*. She cohosts *The Growing Edge* podcast with author Parker J. Palmer. She lives in the wooded hills of southern Indiana with her husband and two shaggy rescue dogs.

Konrad Ng is a cultural curator and organizer who lives in Honolulu, Hawaii. He is executive director of the Shangri La Museum of Islamic Art, Culture & Design, a program of the Doris Duke Charitable Foundation. While he was the director of the Smithsonian Institution's Asian Pacific American Center, he produced the Smithsonian's first exhibition about the history, art, and culture of Asian Pacific America. He marvels at the light of his two daughters and the steady company of his "pandemic" dog. For Konrad, poetry has always been a source of imaginative flight and buoyancy.

Tan Zi Ning is 10 years old as of 2021. She lives in Singapore and is a student at Princess Elizabeth Primary School in Singapore. She managed to play the whole song of Ed Sheeran's "Perfect" on the piano. She enjoys doing art, handicraft, and painting. During 2020, her English teacher taught her how to write poems and she thought it was fun. When she heard about this vaccine poem project, she thought, why not give it a shot? She missed being around friends and didn't like having to wear mask wherever she went. She had to learn online, which has been a challenging task.

TC Nivedita is a 23-year-old literature enthusiast from Kerala, India, with a penchant for writing poetry. She has recently completed her master's in Literatures in English from the English and Foreign Languages University, Hyderabad, with outstanding commendation. Currently she works as a freelance editor. The long days of the pandemic gave her the impetus to ponder over the material, spatial, and literary manifestations of isolation, which she hopes to expand into a doctoral thesis in the near future. Her poem here was also born out of such ruminations and is her first published poem. Poetry offers her respite and inspiration in these trying times.

Grace Nye is a PhD student from Melbourne, Australia. She studies young adult fiction and is working on her first novel. She loves bird-watching and has spotted over 50 different bird species while exploring her neighborhood in lockdown.

Suzanne Ohlmann is a heart failure nurse and writer in South Texas. Her first book, *Shadow Migration*, is being published by University of Nebraska Press in 2022. Her writing can be found on *Longreads* and in *Intima: A Journal of Narrative Medicine*. She and her collaborating cardiologist published a poster and abstract of their rural heart failure program at the 2021 Heart Failure Society of America Annual Scientific Meeting. She lives with her husband and a cadre of dogs and cats in San Antonio, Texas, and Seward, Nebraska, her hometown.

Steven Oscherwitz, MD, is a specialist in infectious diseases, tropical medicine, and epidemiology based in Tuscon, Arizona. He has traveled with archaeologists in the Peten Jungle of Guatemala as an expedition physician and with US government scientists to eradicate parasites in China. Currently Dr. Oscherwitz practices infectious disease medicine and is an associate professor at the University of Arizona College of Medicine, Tucson. Dr. Oscherwitz has been featured on the Discovery Channel's Animal Planet, Discovery Health Channel, local TV, radio programming, and in print media. He enjoys nature, art, poetry, photography, and travel. You can see some of his work here: https://www.pictorem.com/profile/Creative.Endeavors.-.Steven.Oscherwitz.

Lynn Otto is a middle-aged graduate student in Oregon, studying to become a mental health counselor after years of freelancing as an academic copy editor. Her pandemic coping practices include daily dog-walking, hiking when possible, connecting with her kids, and a nightly episode (or three) of whatever TV series she and her husband are both into. Lynn earned an MFA in creative writing from Portland State University in 2013. Her book *Real Daughter: Poems* won a Unicorn Press First Book Award and was a 2020 Oregon Book Awards finalist.

Cristiana Pagliarusco of Vicenza, Italy, is a daughter, a wife, a mother, a sister, an aunt, a teacher, and a friend. She teaches English, and she was proud of herself when she succeeded at gaining her PhD in American poetry. She writes books and poems. She loves what she does—teaching and writing have been her salvation during the lockdowns—and she won't stop doing it if it makes her feel of some use in this wonderful place called Earth.

Nina Palattella is originally from Erie, Pennsylvania, and graduated from Kent State University in 2020. She currently serves as the social media editor for MAYDAY magazine, an editorial assistant for New American Press, and a poetry reader for *Gordon Square Review*. Her fiction and poetry have appeared in *Luna Negra*, *Scribendi*, and *What Rough Beast*. She is editing her first novel and lives in New York City.

Parker J. Palmer is a writer, traveling teacher, and activist who has published ten books and is founder of the Center for Courage & Renewal. At age 82, among his great pleasures are continuing with the at-home part of his work, exploring the woods and waters near his home in Madison, Wisconsin, and being an engaged grandfather in ways that matter. His most recent book is *On the Brink of Everything: Grace, Gravity and Getting Old* (2018). Poetry may well be his religion.

Katherine Willis Pershey is an ordained pastor serving First Congregational Church in Western Springs, Illinois. Her essays have been published in several books as well as in the pages of the *Christian Century*. She and her husband met in a poetry class at Kent State University in 1999. They have two daughters who have inherited their love of books, music, and the Midwest.

Sean Petrie is a teacher, poet, and children's book author in Austin, Texas. He writes poetry on the spot for strangers, on a 1928 Remington Portable, as part of Typewriter Rodeo. He enjoys trees, donuts, and unfiltered laughs. He has two poetry books and high hopes. For more information, please visit www.SeanPetrie.com.

Terri Pilarski is an Episcopal priest in Dearborn, Michigan, serving in a diverse community where the congregation she serves is building a Partnership in Faith with an Arabic speaking congregation.

Hannah Potter is a 27-year-old engineer currently residing in Pasadena, Maryland. She spends time outside work kayaking, endurance cycling, and caring for her dog, two cats, and two chinchillas. This is her first published poem, catching up to her far more accomplished and talented sister, Sarah Gzemski.

Barbara Ras is the author of four poetry collections: *The Blues of Heaven* (Pitt Poetry Series, 2021), *The Last Skin* (Penguin, 2010), which won the Texas Institute of Letters Best Book of 2010, *One Hidden Stuff* (Penguin, 2006), and *Bite Every Sorrow*, which won the Walt Whitman Award and also received the Kate Tufts Discovery Award. She has received fellowships from the Guggenheim and Rockefeller foundations, among others. Ras worked for 40 years in book publishing and is the founding director emerita of Trinity University Press in San Antonio. She now lives in Denver, Colorado.

Anna Mari Räsänen is a poet and painter from Helsinki, Finland. She has written three books of her own and illustrated some books for her friends. For a long time she worked in a small art collective on an island in Helsinki, called Harakka (Magpie). Action Poetry—walks around the island for visitors—was one of her ideas. Another favorite poetic place she likes is a small village in the lake district of Finland, where she now and then travels to spend some forest time with her family and friends.

Gail Rinderknecht lives in Shaker Heights, Ohio, with her husband of 47 years. She is a retired veterinary technician who, in addition to dogs, loves words and reading, knitting, and her grandchildren (not in that order). For years she has enjoyed making books for family and friends which combine her poetry with photographs, but this is her first real published poem.

Dan Rosen lives in Kamakura, Japan, and teaches law at Chuo University in Tokyo. The pandemic has reduced his commuting time from an hour and a half one way to five seconds, since he only needs to get from his bedroom to his computer for online classes. When he is not in front of the screen, he rides his bicycle along the Shonan coast and plays drums, to his neighbors' distress.

Joseph Ross is the author of four books of poetry: *Raising King* (2020), *Ache* (2017), *Gospel of Dust* (2013), and *Meeting Bone Man* (2012). His poems have appeared in the *New York Times Magazine* and in many anthologies and journals. He lives in Washington, DC, and writes regularly at JosephRoss.net.

A physician-writer, **Mo H. Saidi** was born in Iran, moved to the United States, and became an American citizen in 1975. He now lives in San Antonio, Texas, and earned a master's degree in English and American literature and language from Harvard University in 2007. Saidi has published three books of prose, including two novels, and three poetry collections, and a Poetry Society of Texas first-place winner, *Art in the City*. His recent novel, *Esther and the Genius*, was published in 2019.

Jacqueline Saphra is a poet, playwright, literary activist and teacher. Recent publications include *All My Mad Mothers*, shortlisted for the 2017 T. S. Eliot prize, and *Dad, Remember You Are Dead* (2019), both from Nine Arches Press. Her most recent play, *The Noises*, a monologue in the voice of a dog, was shortlisted for a Standing Ovation Award. Her collection *One Hundred Lockdown Sonnets*, written daily, chronicling personal and political upheavals during the first UK lockdown from April to June 2020, was published by Nine Arches Press in 2021. She has four grown-up children, enjoys the incredible alchemy of cake baking, and lives in London.

Mark Scheel is a former Red Cross worker, teacher, editor, and library information specialist residing in the Kansas City, Kansas, region. Now retired, he writes full time. His book *A Backward View: Stories and Poems* was a recipient of the J. Donald Coffin Memorial Book Award from the Kansas Authors Club. His most recent work is the novel *The Potter's Wheel* from Clarendon House Publications, a historical saga of the turbulent sixties in Hollywood, California. He likes to relax by reading contemporary fiction to his wife Dominga while she plays FreeCell on the computer.

Susan Scheid is a poet and literary activist who lives in Washington, DC, with her family and their two cats. Susan has honed her craft while working for the last 30 years as a legal secretary. She was inspired by her father reading poems to her at bedtime and stories of him reading poetry to the other wounded soldiers in the medical hospital during WWII. Her book, *After Enchantment*, was influenced by her love of fairy tales. As a board member, and recently as cochair, for Split This Rock, she has helped bring poetry and activism to thousands of people.

Hailey Schlegel is a recent graduate of Kent State University with a Bachelor's in English and a minor in creative writing. She grew up in Holmesville, Ohio, and is currently living in Kent. She has had short stories and poetry appear in the literary magazines *Luna Negra* and *Brainchild*. Recently, one of her poems was chosen as a winner of the Wayne County Public Library's Imagine Your Story Writing Contest. In her free time, Hailey enjoys reading her growing collection of books, writing, and enjoying the outdoors. Poetry is a relatively new hobby for Hailey, and she thanks everyone at Wick for giving her the confidence to share her work, as well as the opportunity to teach poetry to students in the community. Hailey lost her grandma to COVID in December and dedicates her poem to her memory.

Sadie Schlegel is from Holmesville, Ohio, but currently lives in Kent, Ohio. She is a 2021 Kent State University graduate with a Bachelor's in English and a minor in creative writing. She had two of her short stories published in the spring 2020 editions of *Brainchild* and *Luna Negra* literary arts magazines. She enjoys reading and writing while cuddling with her cat Zig-Zag. Sadie has been involved with the Wick Poetry

Center during her time at Kent State University and she thanks them for growing her love of poetry. The pandemic has hit Sadie's family rather hard several times, and she wishes to dedicate her poem in this anthology to her grandma, Karen Lilley.

Bonnie James Shaker, PhD, is associate professor of English at Kent State University's Geauga Campus where she teaches composition, literature, and media studies. Although born and raised in northeast Ohio where she and her husband also raised their family, she has published, researched, and lectured across the United States and in Europe on the author Kate Chopin. With the exception of a sixth-grade limerick contest and her undergraduate school student newspaper, this is her first published poem.

Peggy Shumaker has taught creative writing since 1976. She served as Alaska's Writer Laureate. Her most recent book is *Cairn, New and Selected Poems and Prose*. Right now, she is learning to do her husband Joe's dialysis at her home in Fairbanks, Alaska.

Michael Simms is a community activist who lives in Pittsburgh, Pennsylvania. His proudest accomplishment has been to help found the Waldorf School of Pittsburgh. His books of poems include *American Ash* and *Nightjar*, both published by Ragged Sky Press. He enjoys taking walks in the woods with his dog Josie while foraging for wild plants and herbs.

Kashiana Singh is a management professional by job classification and a work practitioner by personal preference. Kashiana's TEDx talk was dedicated to her life mantra of Work as Worship. Her poetry collection, *Shelling Peanuts and Stringing Words*, presents her voice as a participant and an observer. Her second chapbook, *Crushed Anthills*, is a collection of poems and photographs through which she unravels her journey through ten cities. Her poems have been published on various platforms. She is a regular voice on the Wednesday Night Poetry Series run by Kai Coggin and is very proud to have been a featured poet for their Inauguration Day event. Kashiana lives in Chicago, is moving to North Carolina, and carries her various geographical homes within her poetry. She serves as a managing editor for *Poets Reading the News* and is working on her second full-length collection, *Woman by the Door*.

Emily-Sue Sloane is a poet who lives in Huntington Station, New York. Her poems have appeared in a variety of journals and anthologies and have won awards, including first place in the Nassau County Poet Laureate Society 2021 Poetry Contest. After retiring from a career in magazine and journal publishing, she resumed a long dormant writing practice, which helps her appreciate life, especially in a pandemic. In addition to writing, she enjoys reading, daily walks, and practicing yoga. Her first full-length book, *We Are Beach Glass*, is due out in early 2022. For more information, please visit www.emilysuesloane.com.

Kelley Alison Smith is a feminist Unitarian Universalist Alto II living in northern Rhode Island who works for Brown University. She is also a creative nonfiction writer who is slowly working on a memoir about falling in love with the South Pacific and having to leave due to a brain tumor diagnosis. For many years she was a backstage manager and emcee at the Newport Folk Festival. She is an avid amateur naturalist who enjoys birding, snorkeling, and being with her loved ones. She can't wait to be singing with others again soon.

Todd Snider currently resides in Munroe Falls, Ohio, with his wife, Jennifer, his three children, Cameron, Griffin, and Addison, and a rescue dog named Dorsett. He has worked in advertising and marketing for over 20 years and has spent the last three years working in marketing for Kent State University. Todd, who is an avid bourbon drinker, loves to travel and spends a lot of time supporting and watching his kids do amazing things. During the pandemic, Todd and his family took advantage of the isolation time and the need to be safe by renting an RV and traveling cross country to see all the amazing places our country has to offer. This is his first published poem.

Sue Soal is a social process facilitator and evaluator working for public benefit with community organizations, research initiatives, and public sector projects. She lives in Muizenberg, a windy seaside suburb in Cape Town, South Africa, surrounded by mountain, sea, and wetland. Sue enjoys reading poetry—especially modern American poets—and writing small vignettes. She is the mom of an adult son who is a musician and economist.

Barbara Solow is a former newspaper reporter now working in higher education. She still wears her reporter's hat as she goes through life, maintaining a desire to bear witness and engage with other people. She is grateful to have stayed employed and healthy thus far during the pandemic. She is also thankful for her community in western Massachusetts, which is full of radical forebears and standup citizens. In her after-work hours, she is learning French and tai chi sword. Her biggest source of hope and strength is her family, most notably her husband and son.

Kate Sommers-Dawes lives in San Francisco, California, where she works as a freelance journalist. The COVID-19 pandemic, while arduous in so many ways, inspired her to start swimming in the reliably chilly but rejuvenating San Francisco Bay. Kate is married to a world-traveling surfer who taught her to backpack the Yosemite wilderness, now her happy place. She is mother to an adventurous toddler who makes friends wherever he goes. Every day he is a reminder that each of us is born a poet.

Cathy Song is a Hawai'i-born poet who has lived most of her life on Oahu and Hawai'i Islands. The author of five books of poetry including *Picture Bride* (Yale Younger Poets Prize) and the recipient of the Hawai'i Award for Literature, her latest publication, *All the Love in the World*, is a short story collection. She began writing "Yellow Peril" when news of a mysterious virus in Wuhan, China, began to circulate. As the grandchild of immigrants who came to Hawai'i in the late 1800s, she grew up knowing the long sad history of Asian racism in the West.

Kim Stafford lives in Portland, Oregon, where he retired from Lewis & Clark College after teaching there for 40 years, and also in Italy, Scotland, Mexico, and Bhutan. He is the author of *Singer Come from Afar*, and during the pandemic posted poems of consolation daily on Instagram.

Melissa Standish is a grandmother who lives in Houston, Texas. She has practiced psychotherapy for over 30 years and is interested in the human journey and the inner life revealed in dreams, nature, and the spiritual life. She and her husband of 49 years look forward to enjoying time with family and friends, near and far.

Jan Stretch is a retired psychiatric nurse-therapist from Victoria, British Columbia, Canada. A highlight of her career was codeveloping a national mental health training program for physicians. She continues to support friends, some of whom are struggling with serious illness. Jan enjoys her large extended family, especially her two grandchildren. She returned to thoughts of poetry on her daily walks in the park, creating her first of many haiku in early 2021. Insights gained from her walks helped create this work of her pandemic experience. This is her first published poem.

Ellyse Theede is a mother, wife, and teacher who lives on Treaty 6 territory in Saskatoon, Saskatchewan, Canada. She has been an English language arts yeacher in Outlook, Saskatchewan, since 2012. Her greatest joy and inspiration is her family. Ellyse always tries to lead a life of kindness and stewardship. This is her first published poem.

Mosab Abu Toha is a bilingual Palestinian poet, fiction writer, and essayist who was raised in a refugee camp in Gaza. He is the father of three beautiful kids. From 2019 to 2020, Mosab was a visiting poet at Harvard's Department of Comparative Literature. In 2017, Mosab founded the Edward Said Public Library, the first English language library in Gaza, which now has two branches. Mosab teaches English at UNRWA schools in Gaza, and his first poetry book will be published in 2022 by City Lights Books. Mosab loves to take photos, either with words or his phone, of the sea, the sunset, and flowers. However, he cannot ignore pictures of destruction around him. When the pandemic hit Gaza, he couldn't take the vaccine because of the border closures and was later delayed and couldn't leave Gaza in time for a program in the United States.

Erkut Tokman is a Turkish poet, actor, visual artist, editor, and translator and lives in İstanbul. He studied poetry, modern dance, and acting in London, Bucharest, and Milan. He is a member of Turkish and İtaly PEN Centers working for WiPC (Writers in Prison Committee) and founder of AÇIK ŞİİR movement based on performance poetry. He writes for Artfulliving.com.tr and Ters Dergi. He has five poetry books. He won the İtalian Ministry of Culture Translation Award in 2019 as well as the Messina Citta di Arta and Salvotore Quasimodo Jaci Poetry Awards.

TC Tolbert (he/him/hey grrrl) of Tuscon, Arizona, is a trans and genderqueer monkey-goat who never ceases to experience a simultaneous grief and deep love any time s/he pays attention to the world. S/he writes poems, works with wood, learns, teaches, and wanders. In 2019, TC was awarded an Academy of American Poets' Laureate Fellowship for his work with trans, nonbinary, and queer folks as Tucson's Poet Laureate. For more information, please visit www.tctolbert.com.

Susan M. Tyrrell lives in Texas and is an associate professor of English at Cameron University in Lawton, Oklahoma. She writes features locally for *580 Monthly* and has recently finished her memoir, *Stateless*, about growing up in the United States as an adopted orphan from Palestine. She also writes poetry around themes about the Palestinian diaspora.

Prasanta Verma is a freelance writer and poet. She was born under an Asian sun, raised in the Appalachian foothills in the South, and resides in Milwaukee, Wisconsin. She holds an MBA and an MPH, and her poetry has been published or is forthcoming in *Relief Journal*, *Barren Magazine*, *Tweetspeak Poetry*, *Bramble Lit Mag*, and a *New York Quarterly* anthology. She enjoys writing and creating. You can connect with her on Twitter @ VermaPrasanta and her website prasantaverma.com

Ann N. Vermel directs Readers' Theatre in Fort Collins, Colorado, and writes wherever she is. She retired from a long career in nonprofit arts management and now works to raise funds for rural school districts in California and Colorado. Her poems have been published in small journals and a few anthologies.

Sandra Villeneuve lives in Ontario, Canada, where she works in retail and does custom sewing and cosplay design. She calls herself a feral housewife and loves to lose track of time in the garden and other creative pursuits.

Stephanie Vincent is originally from New Castle, Pennsylvania, but now resides in Kent, Ohio, where she is a part-time instructor in the Department of History at Kent State University. She has previously published articles about business history and the pottery industry and has contributed to an edited volume about the Civilian Conservation

Corps at the Virginia Kendall Reserve at Cuyahoga Valley National Park, but this is her first published poem. In her spare time, she enjoys crafting, reading, and spending time with family.

Ken Waldman of Anchorage, Alaska, combines original poetry, Appalachian-style string-band music, and smart storytelling for a performance uniquely his. Since 1995, he's appeared at the widest range of venues, from the Kennedy Center Millennium Stage to the Dodge Poetry Festival to the Woodford Folk Festival (Queensland, Australia). His 19 books consist of 16 full-length poetry collections, a memoir (about life on tour), a creative writing manual, and a kids' book. His nine CDs include two for children. In 2022, Cyberwit Press of India will publish his novel, *Now Entering Alaska Time*, set in Fairbanks, Juneau, and Nome, communities where he's lived. His vaccine? Two Pfizer shots.

Hannah Jane Walker is a poet, playwright, and author who lives in Essex, United Kingdom. She makes work about the difficult uplifting process of being a person and often works with marginalized groups facilitating writing workshops. She has published numerous poems. Life during the pandemic has consisted of home schooling and writing her first nonfiction book, *Sensitive*.

Tracy Rice Weber is the author of the chapbook *All That Keeps Me*, released in 2021 from Finishing Line Press. She received an MFA from Old Dominion University and is on the adjunct English faculty there. Her work has been published in *River*, *Bangalore Review*, and *Barely South Review*, as well as others. She lives with her husband and sons in Coastal Virginia.

Claire Weiner is a recently retired clinical social worker in Ann Arbor, Michigan. She began seeing all her patients virtually when the pandemic began. As difficult as this time has been for humanity, there is still something about the human spirit that is resilient and awe inspiring. She began writing when her children left home.

Kari Wimbish is a middle school humanities teacher in Charlotte, North Carolina. Teaching during the COVID-19 pandemic affirmed her confidence in the resilience of adolescents and in the dedication of her colleagues. This is her first published poem.

Warren Woessner is a poet, attorney, and avid birder from Minneapolis, Minnesota. He has published widely, and the most recent of his six collections of poetry is Exit–Sky (Holy Cow! Press). He has received fellowships in poetry from the NEA, the Wisconsin Arts Board, and the McKnight Foundation, and won the Minnesota Voices Competition. He splits his time between Minneapolis and Martha's Vineyard, where he is on the Board of the Vineyard Conservation Society.

Laura Wood is a retired businesswoman who splits her time between Owen Sound and Toronto, Ontario. She has founded two local community groups: electHER (to promote gender equality in local municipal politics) and Owen Sound Waste Watchers (educating others about moving to a lower-impact lifestyle). When she gets a spare minute, Laura loves spending time with family, including a new grandson, Wyatt, and singing in choirs. This is her first published poem, and she thanks Naomi Shihab Nye for the inspiration.

Nisreen Yamany is a Kent State University alum with a PhD degree in English literature. In the summer of 2021, she moved back to her home country, Saudi Arabia, and to her job as an academic at Umm Al-Qura University in Makkah. She has been writing poetry for years and was glad to volunteer as a teaching artist at Old Trail School in the Cuyahoga Valley, in addition to leading an online poetry workshop. During the pandemic, she felt grateful that she was in Kent and didn't experience the lockdown that her family experienced in Saudi Arabia. Instead, she could freely roam the green parks and visit the Cuyahoga River.

Caitie Young is a poet and fiction writer in Kent, Ohio. Their poetry has appeared in Luna Negra, Welter (online), and the Santa Fe Writers Project. They enjoy true crime podcasts and spending time with their cat, Cami. Caitie is also passionate about protecting transgender youth and queer activism. Throughout the pandemic, they worked as a front desk agent at a hotel which greatly influenced their work. Caitie is pursuing their MFA in poetry through the Northeast Ohio Master of Fine Arts Program.

Dr. **Ofelia Zepeda** is Tohono O'odham. She is currently a Regents Professor of Linguistics at the University of Arizona and is the recipient of a MacArthur Fellowship for her work in American Indian language education, maintenance, and recovery. She is the author of *A Tohono O'odham Grammar*, the first pedagogical grammar on the language. As a poet she writes both in O'odham and English and has published three books of poetry, *Ocean Power: Poems from the Desert*, *Jewed I-hoi: Earth Movements*, and *Where Clouds Are Formed*. She enjoys being outside in the desert around Tucson.